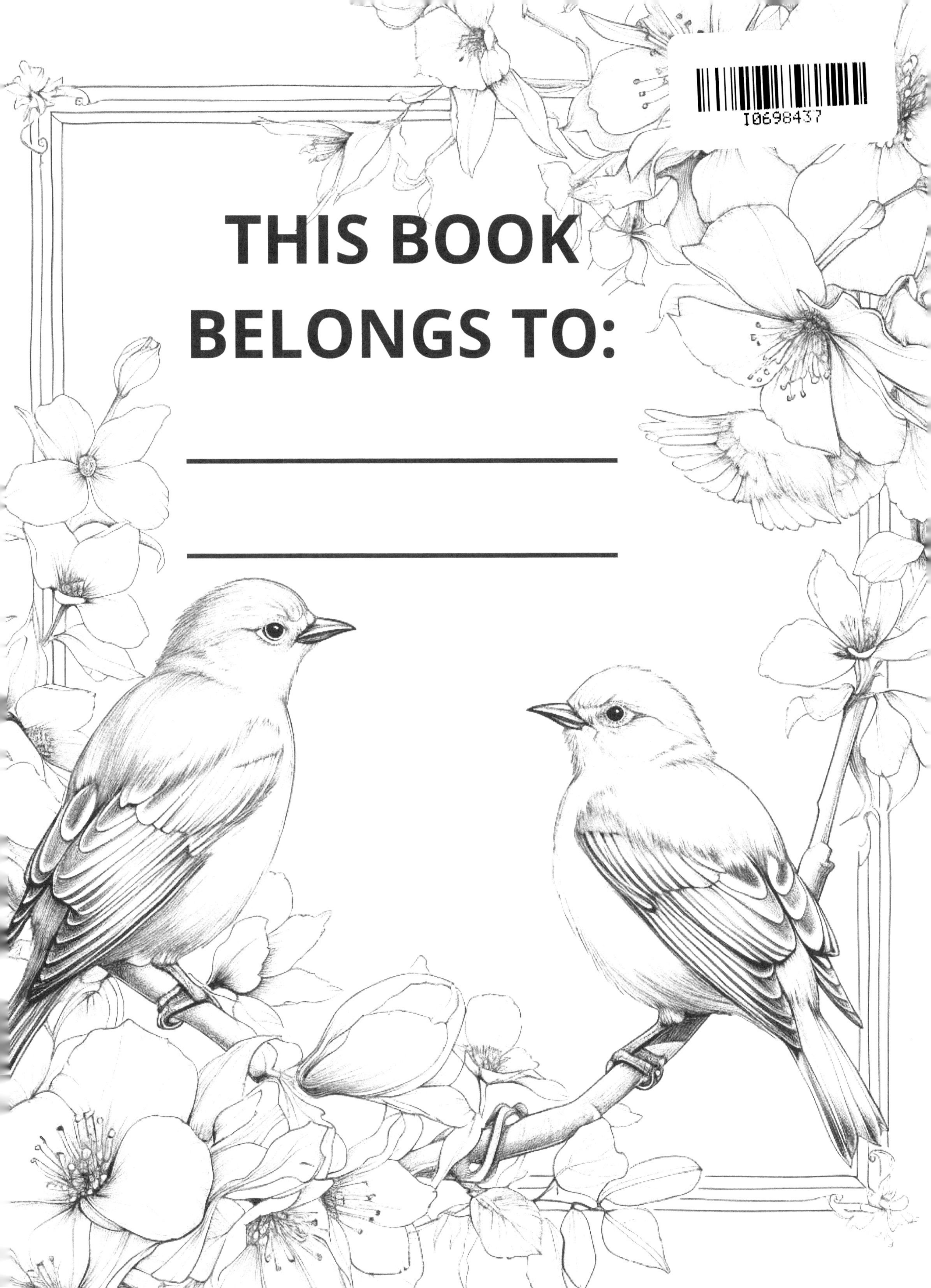

THIS BOOK
BELONGS TO:

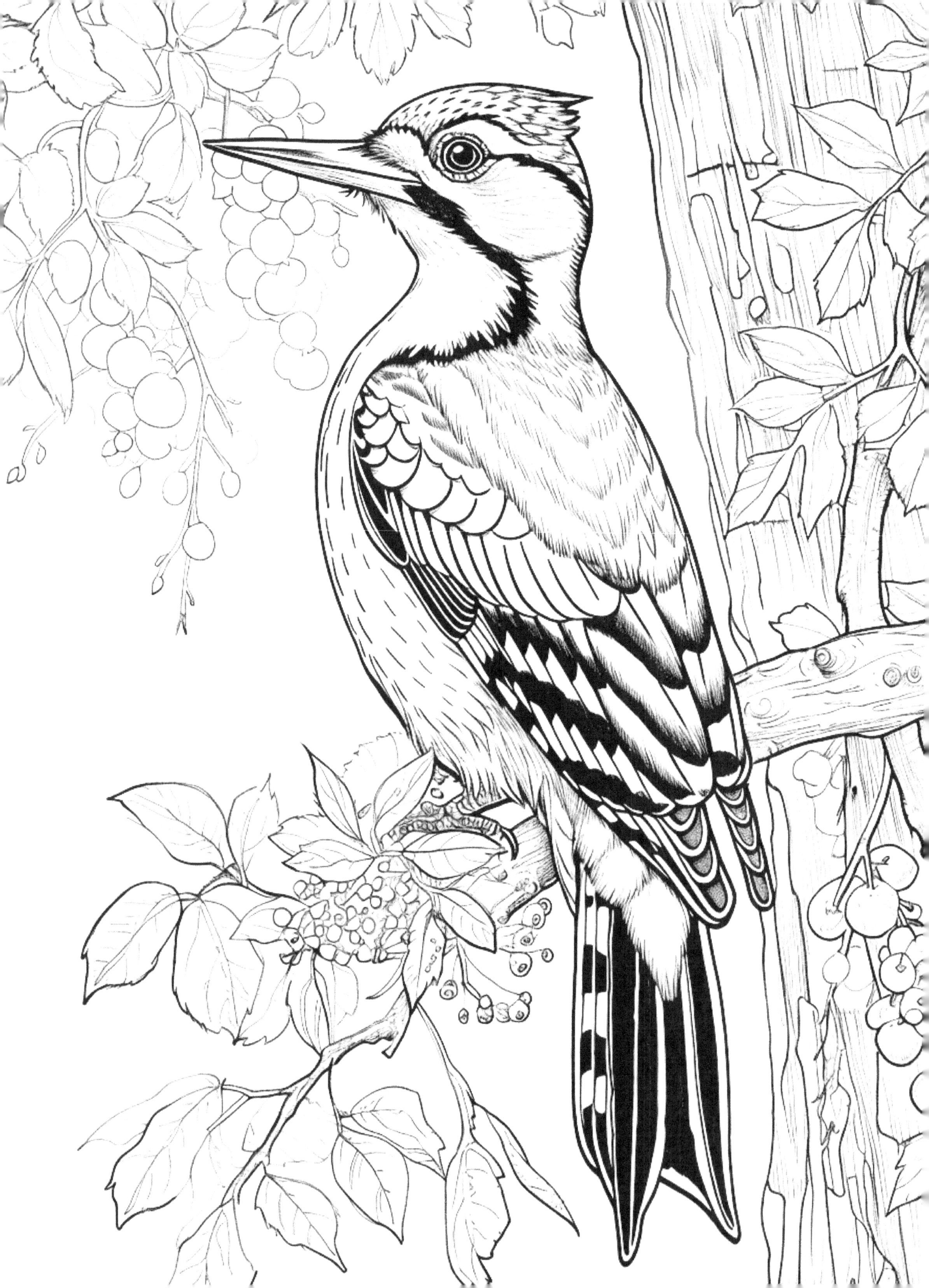

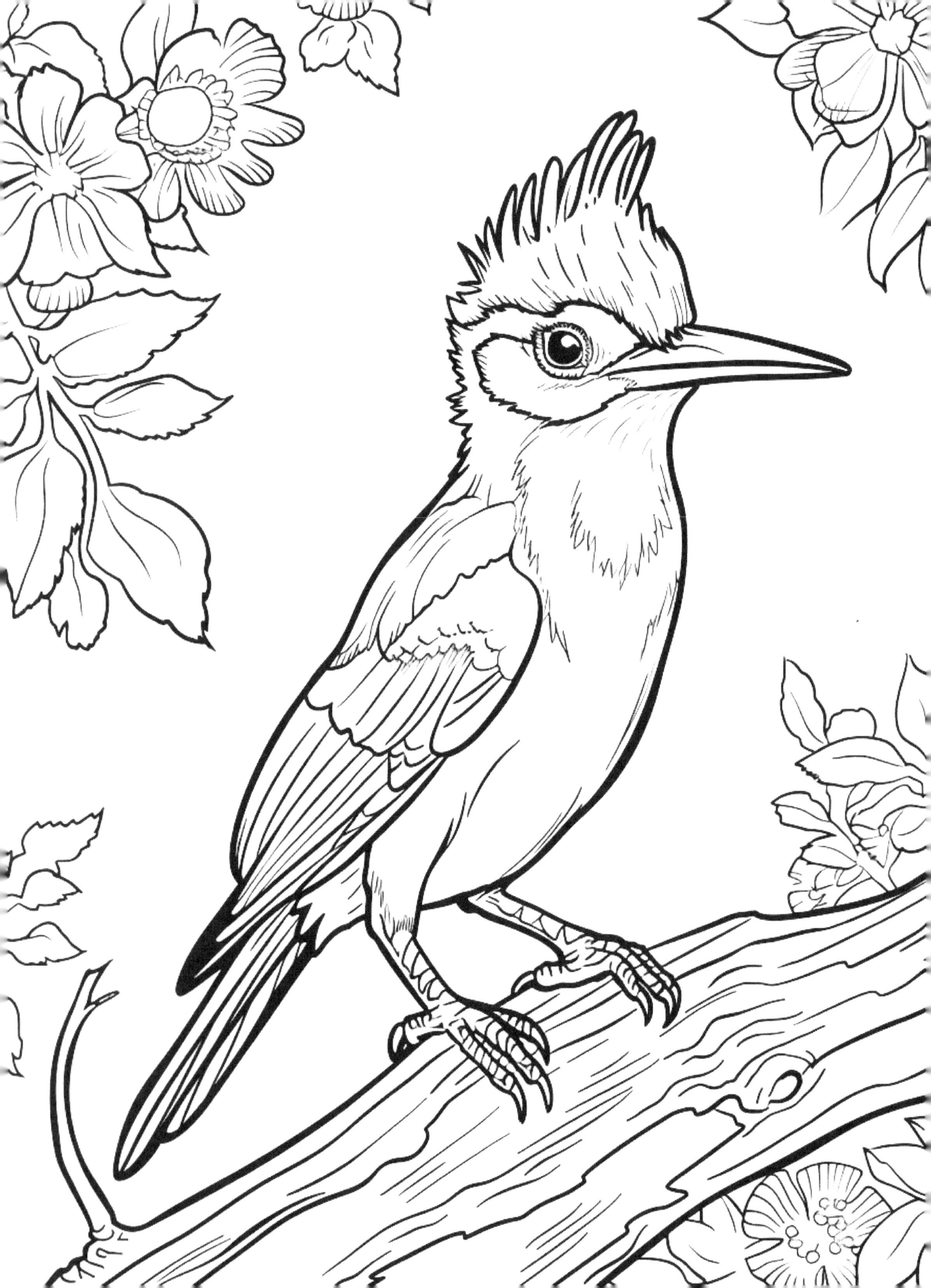

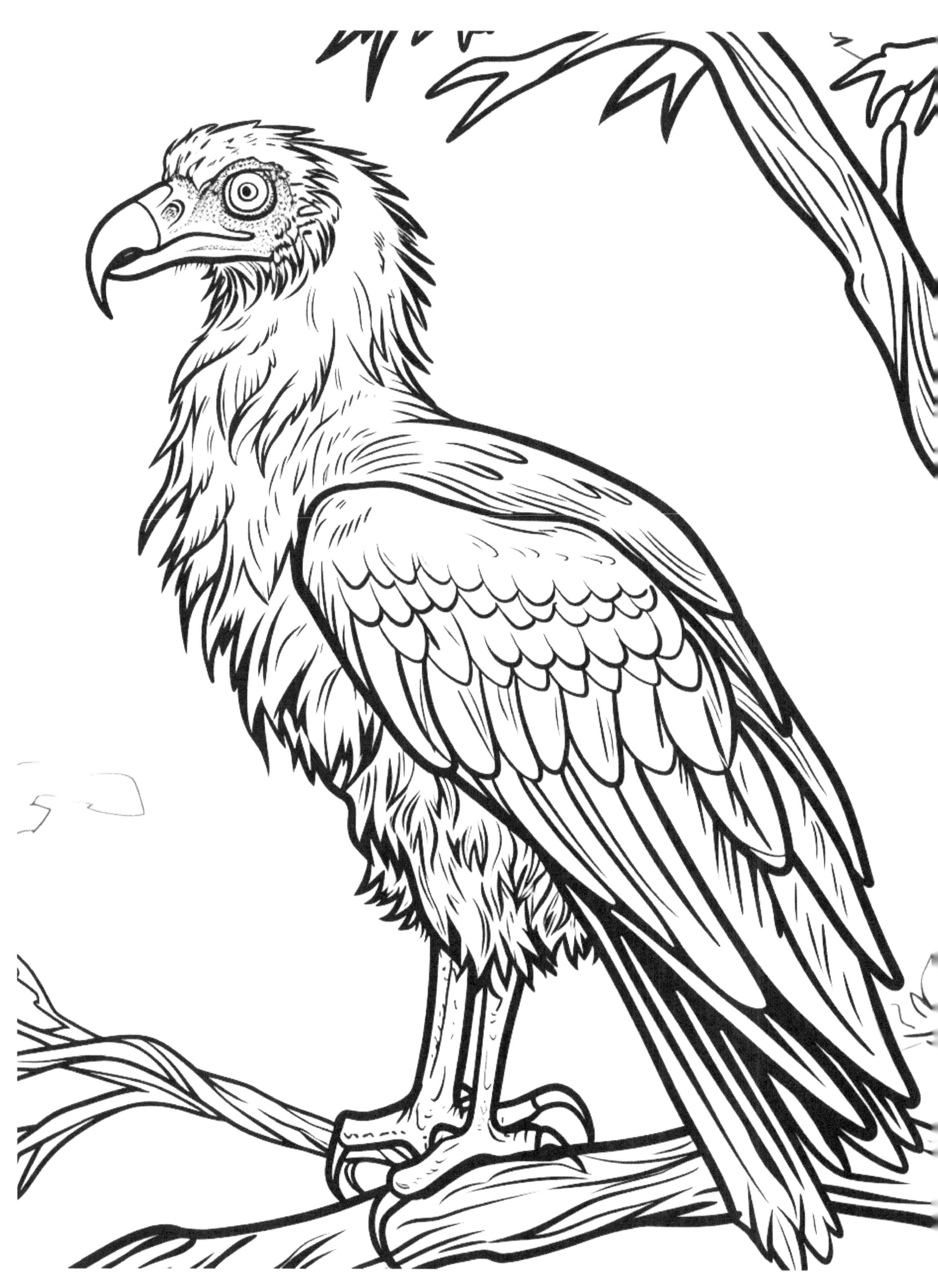

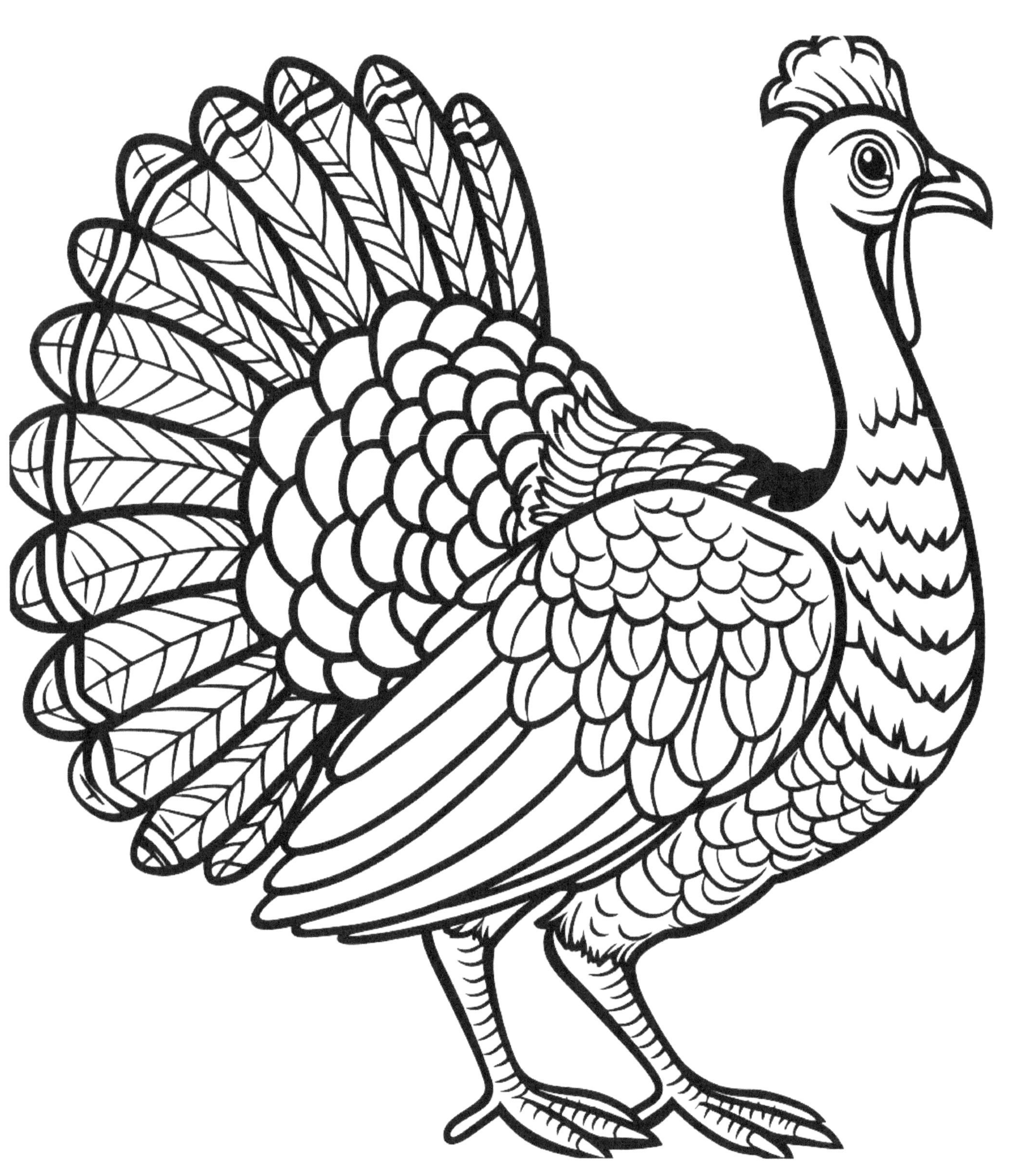

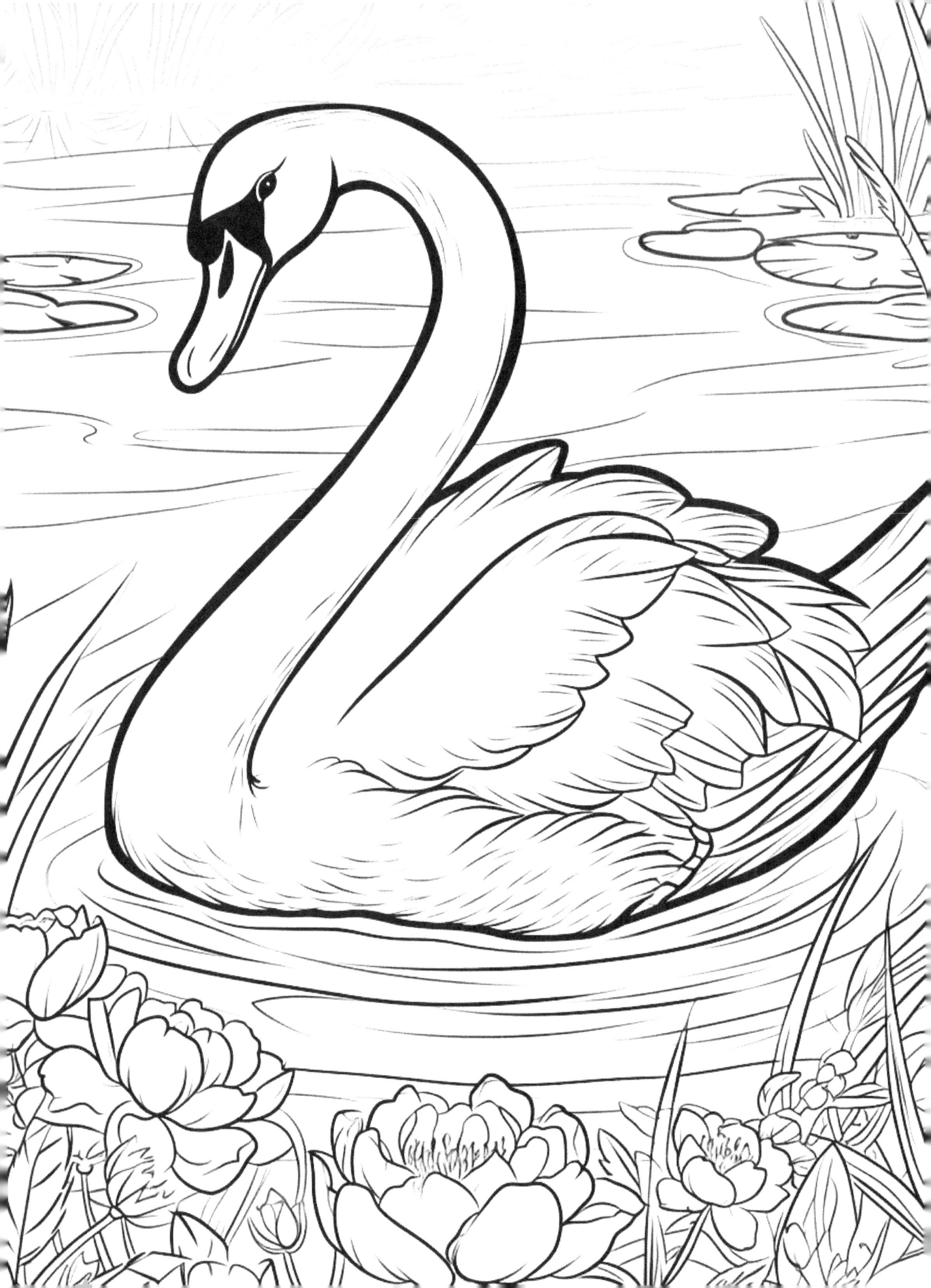

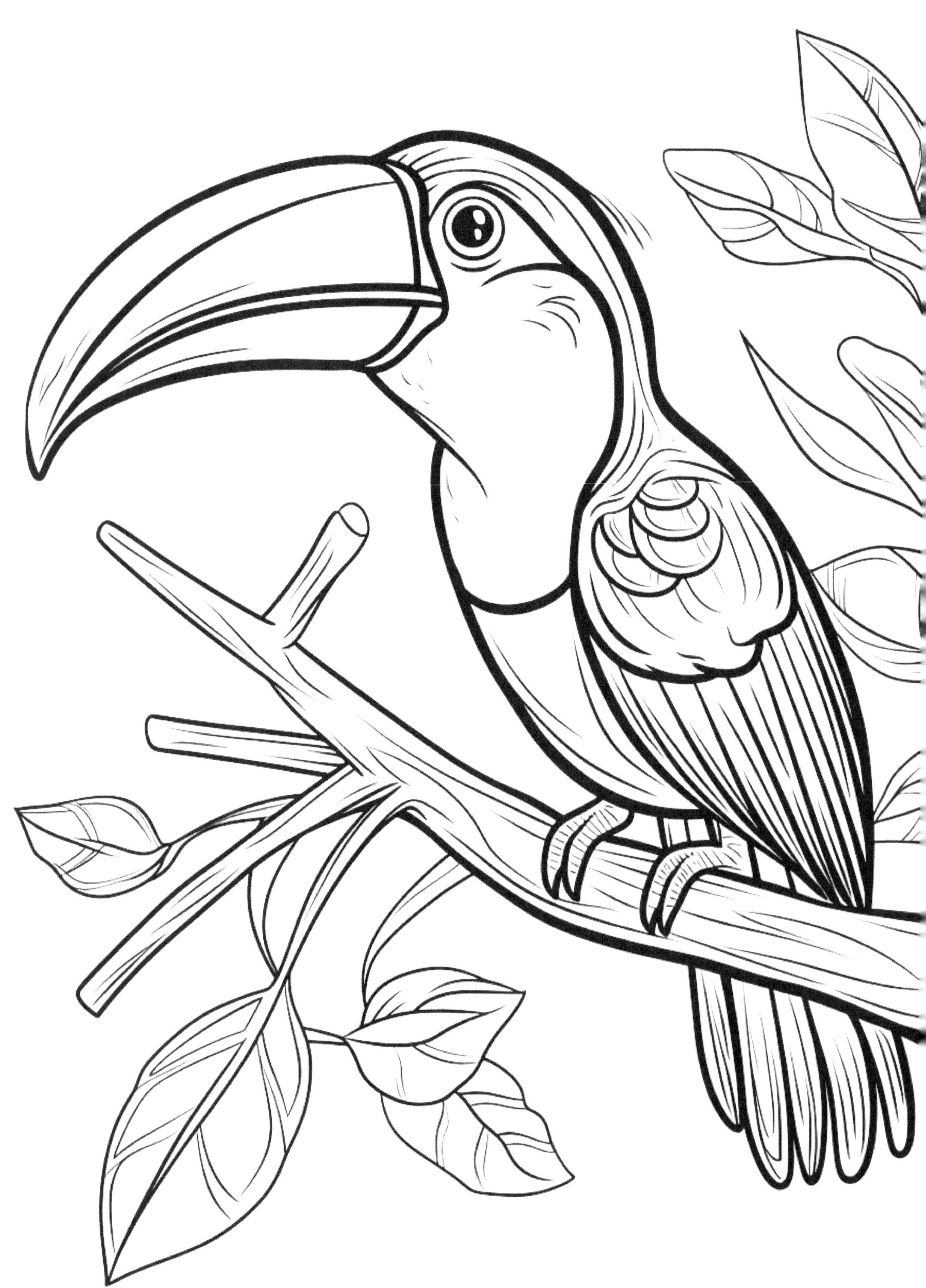

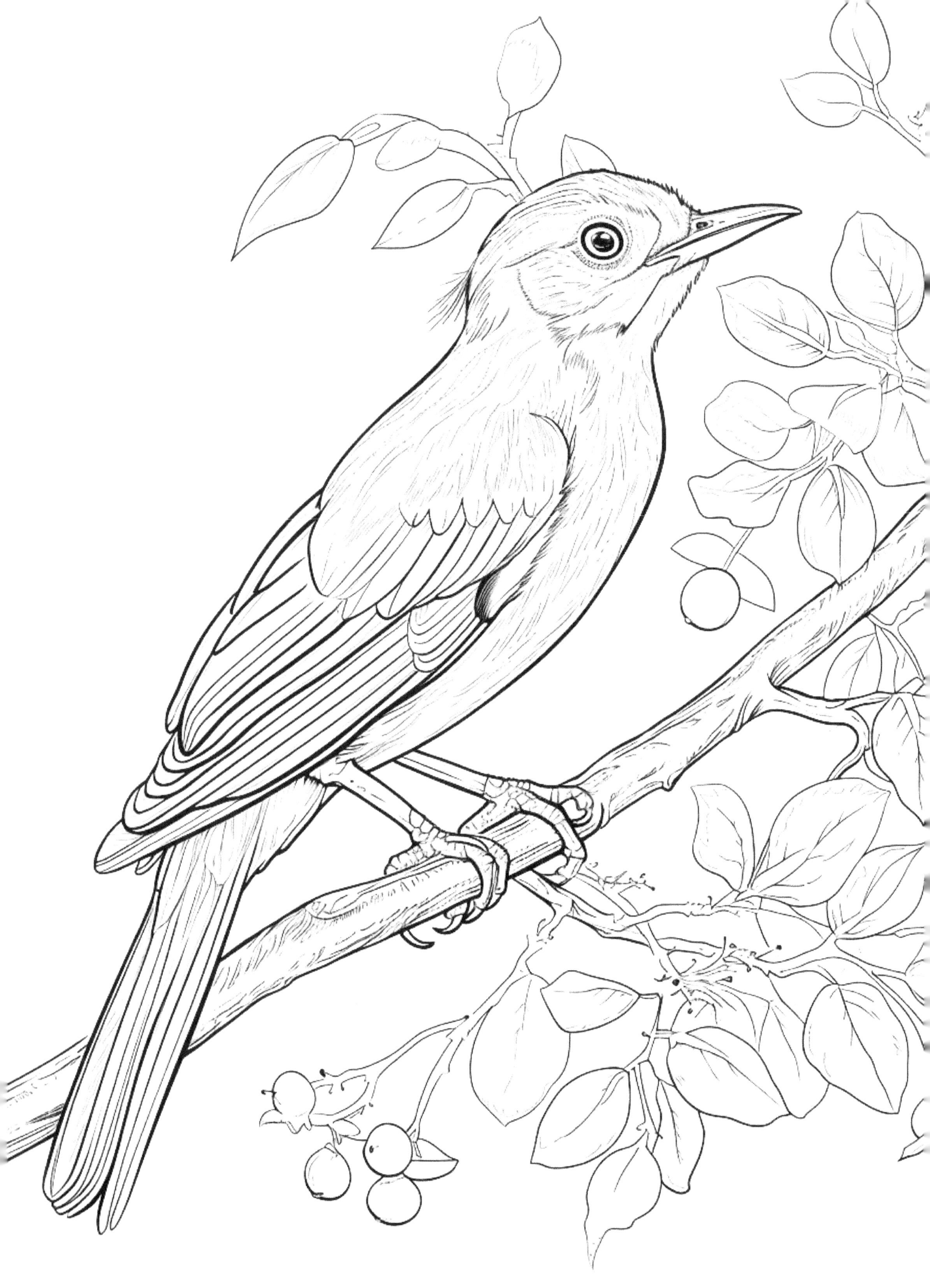

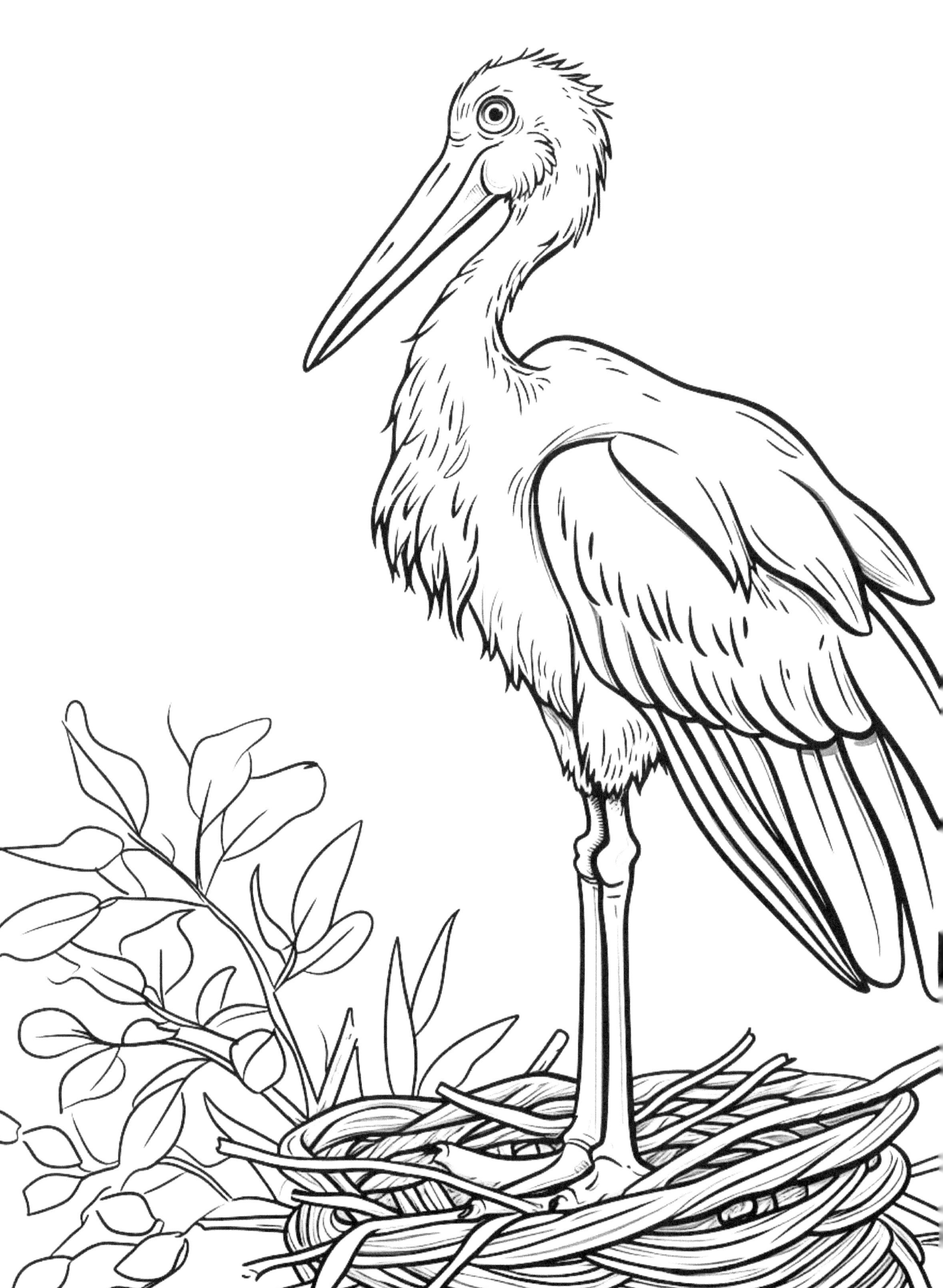

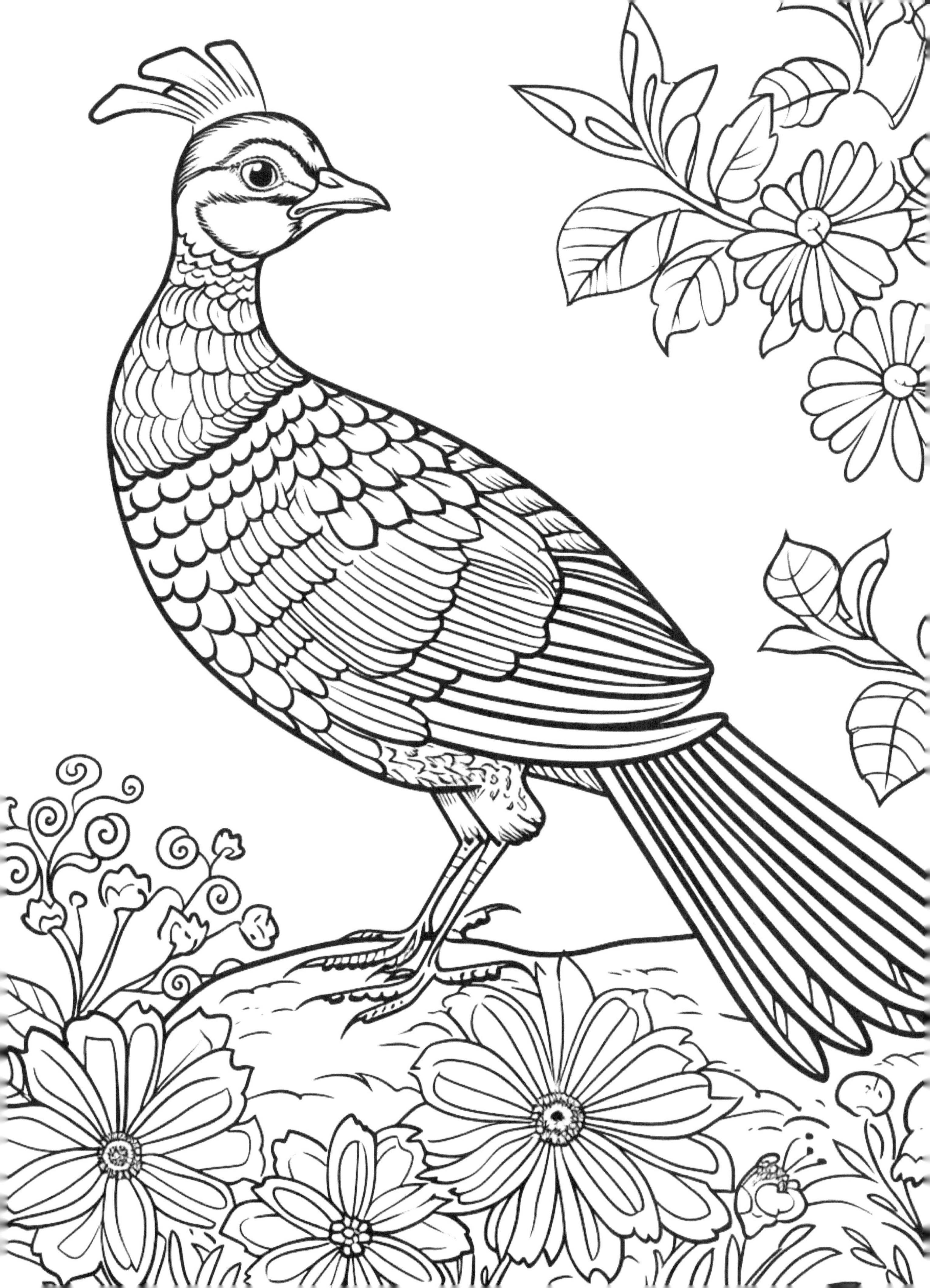

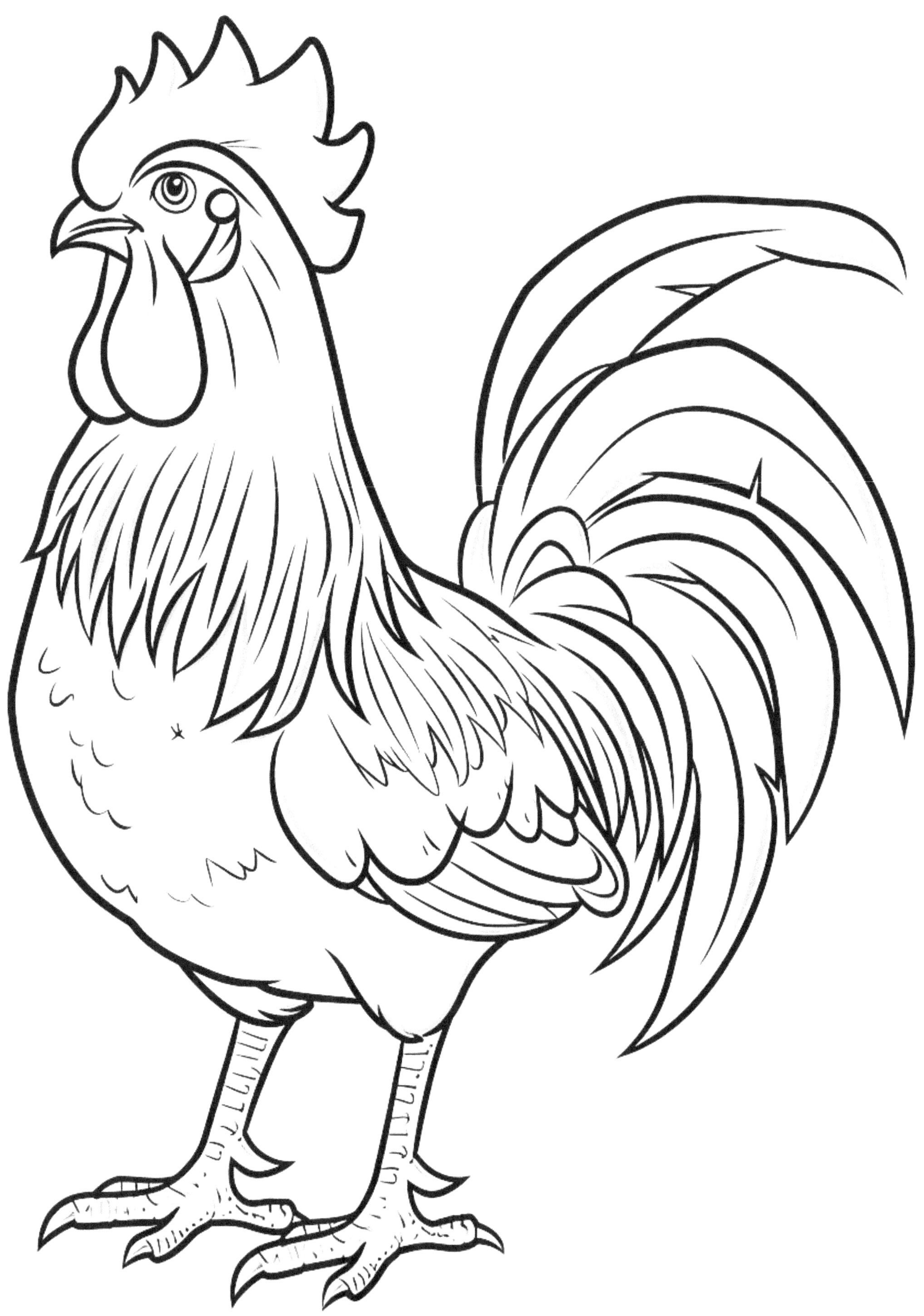

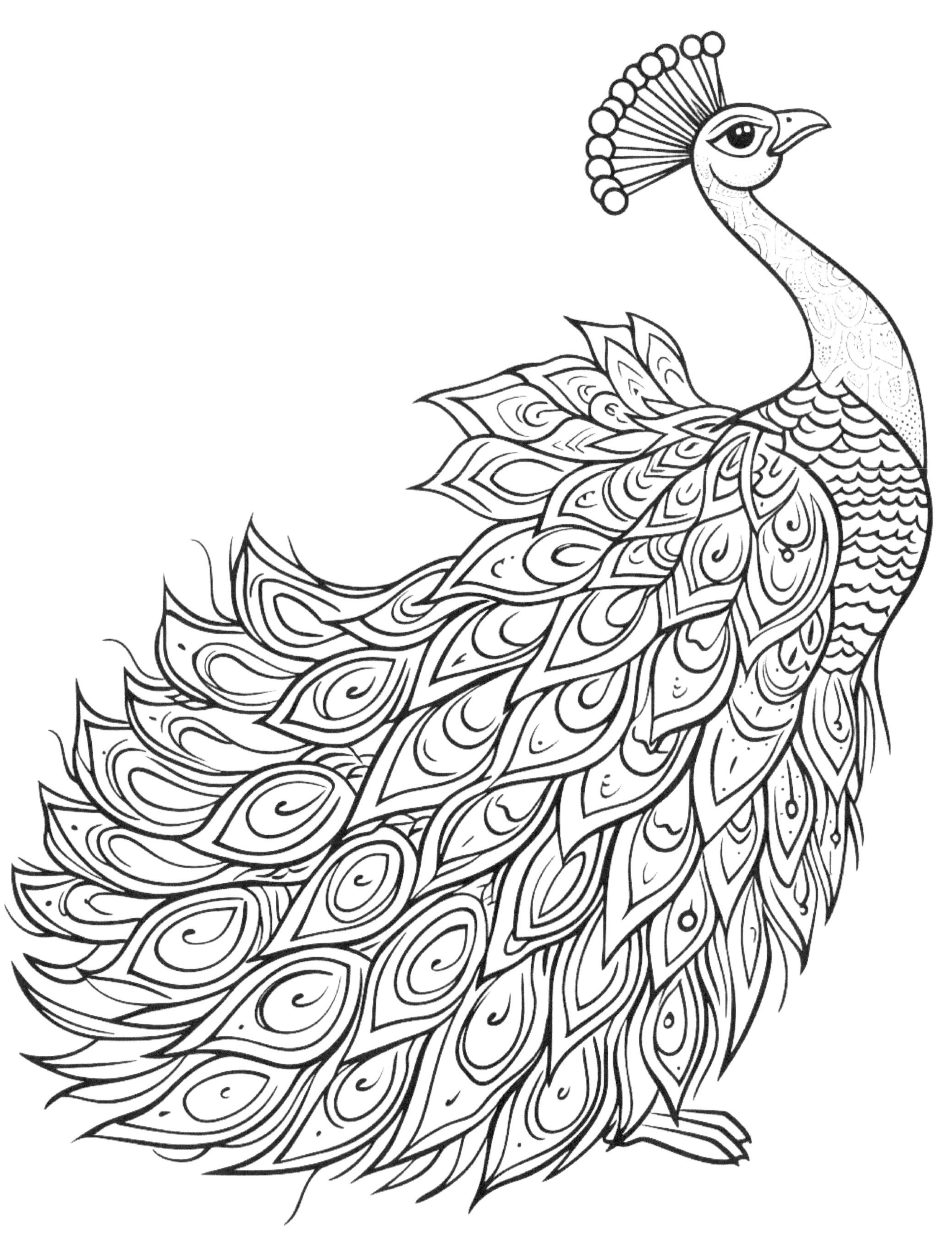

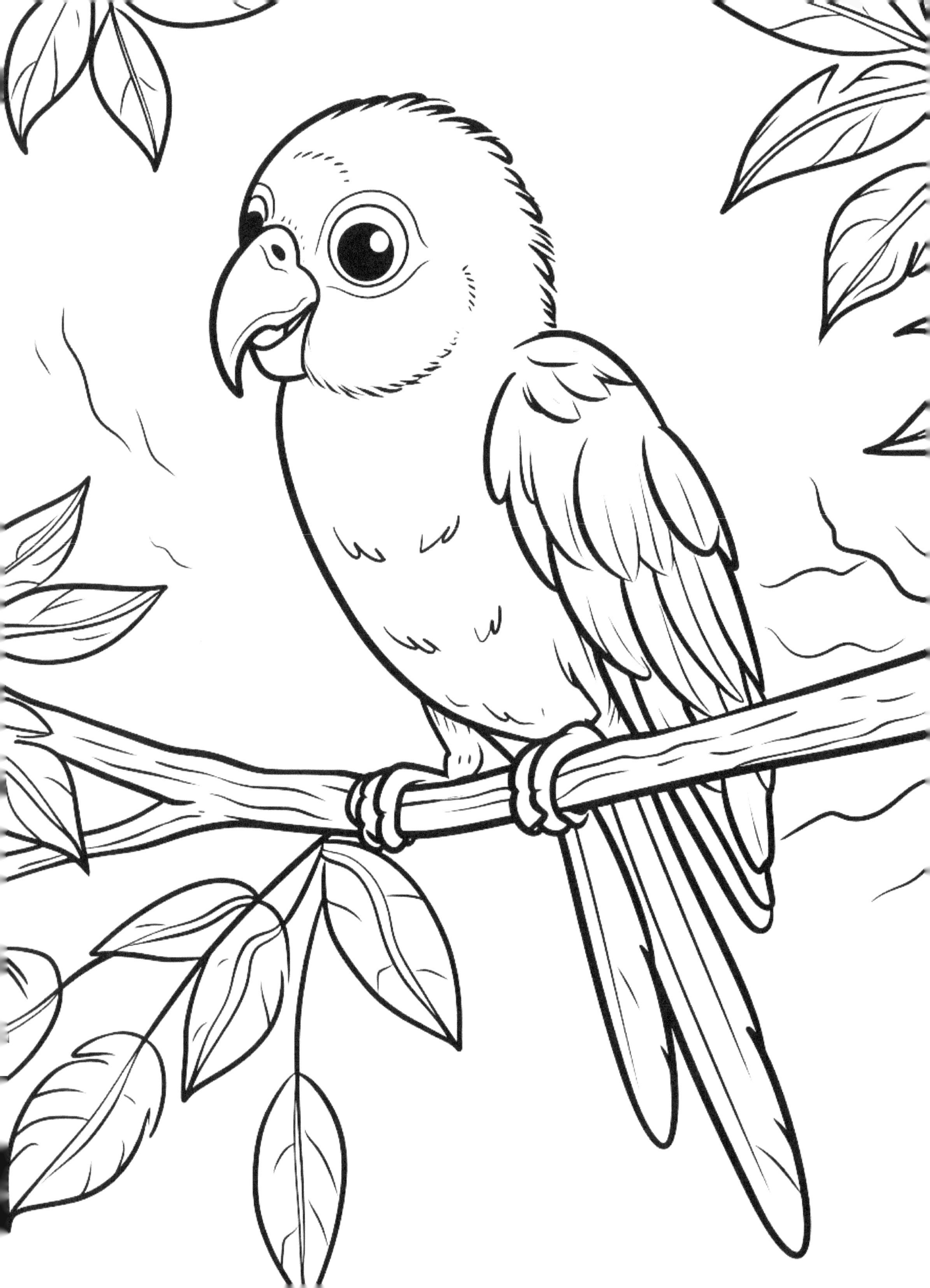

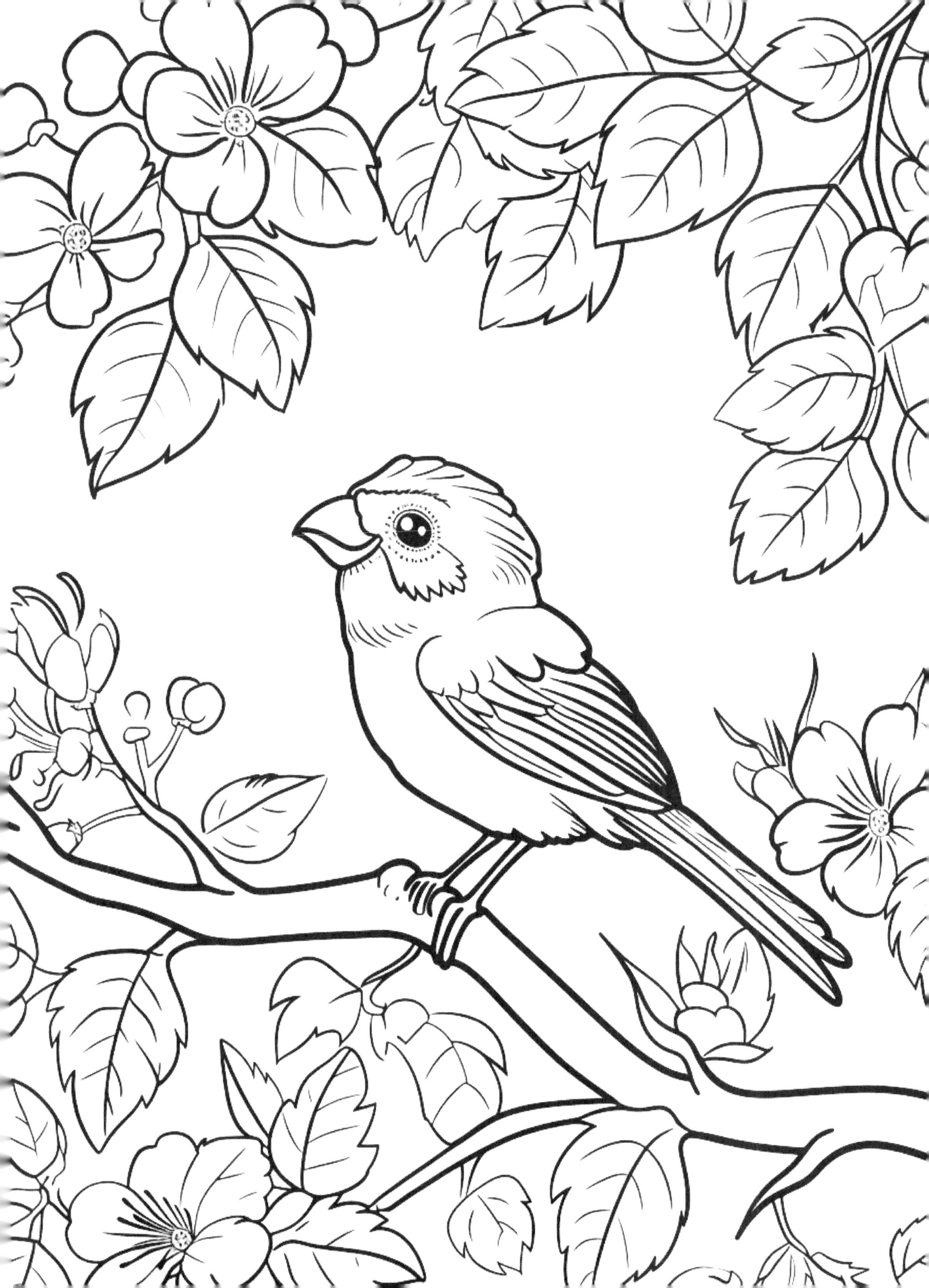

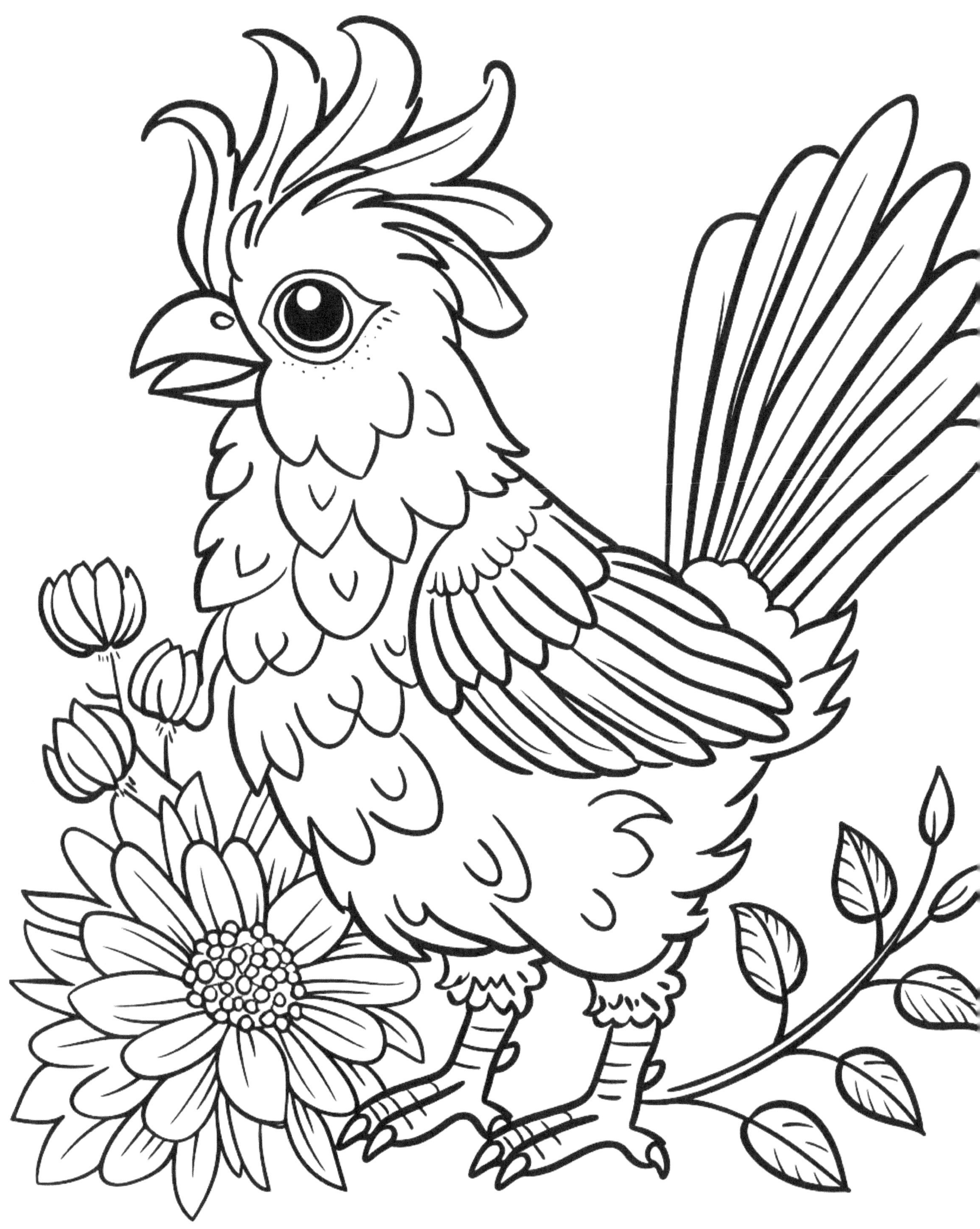

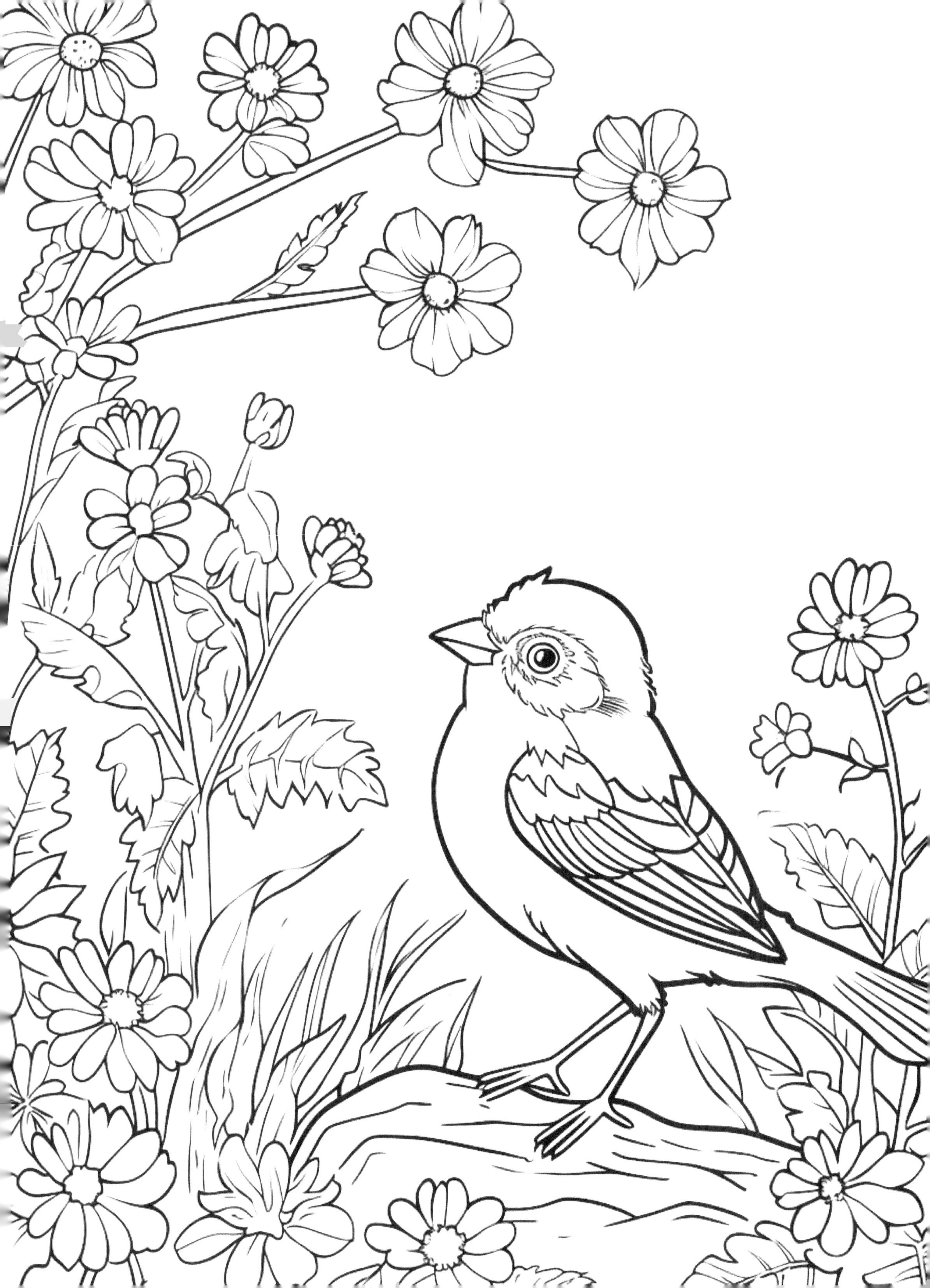

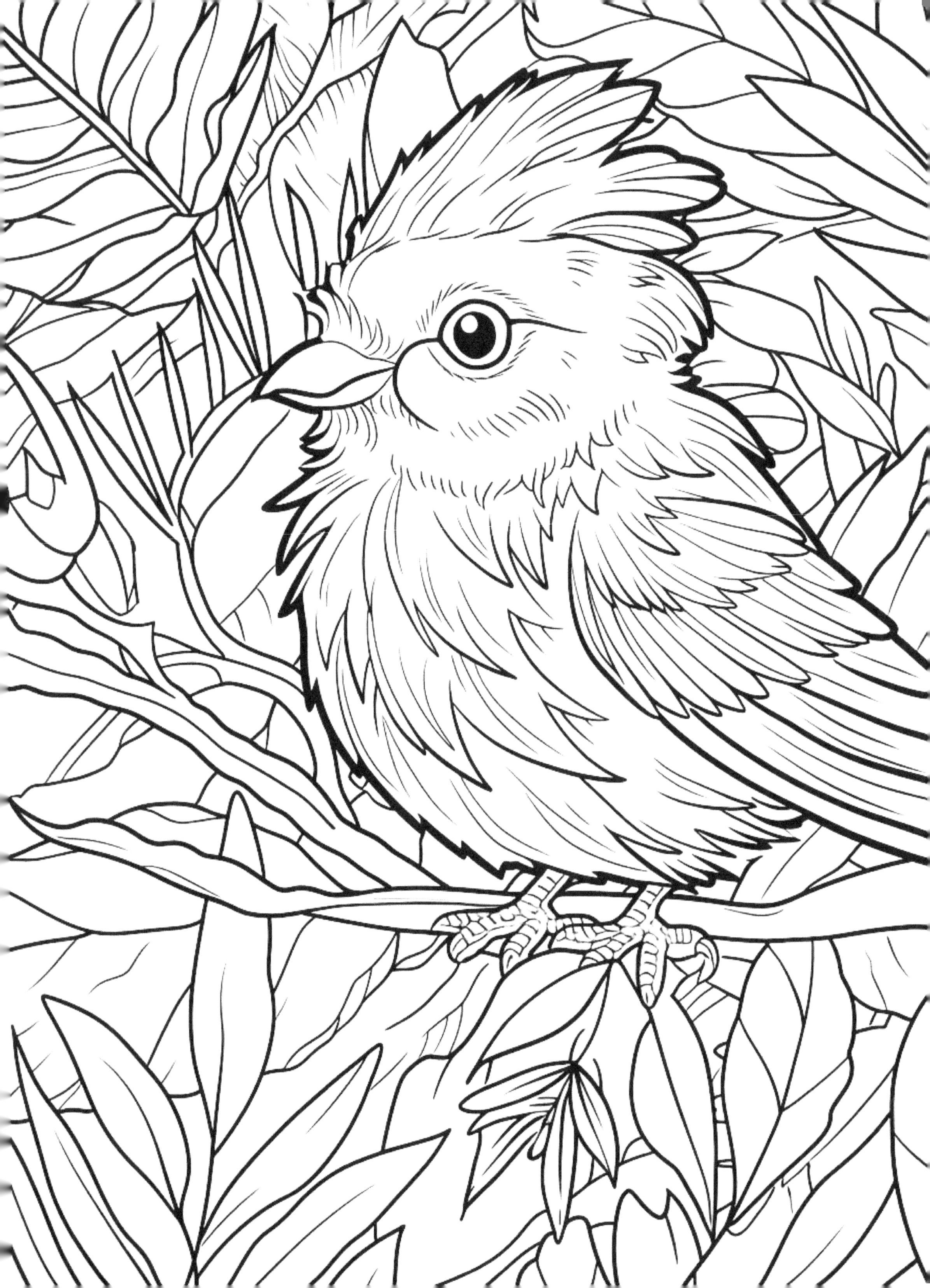

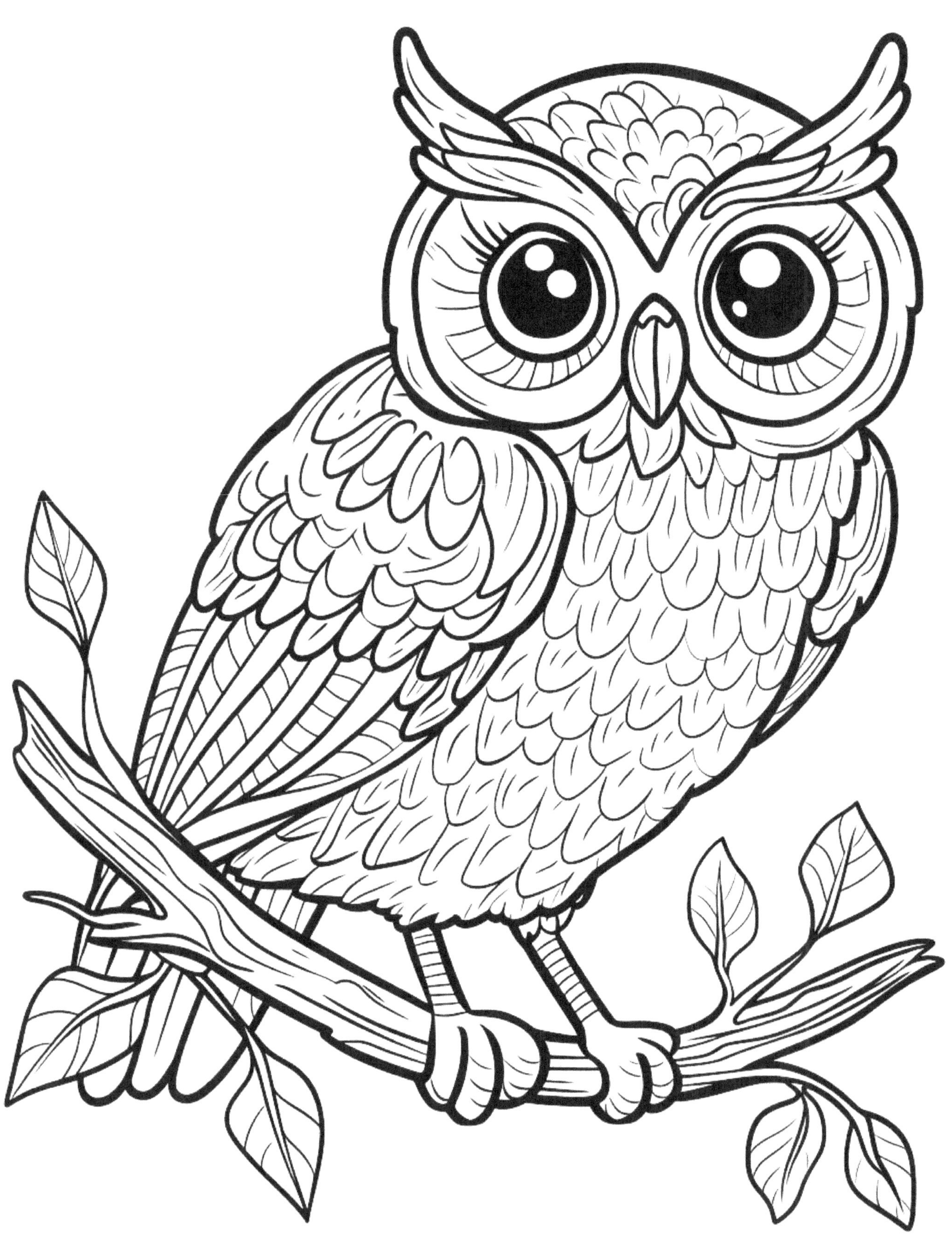

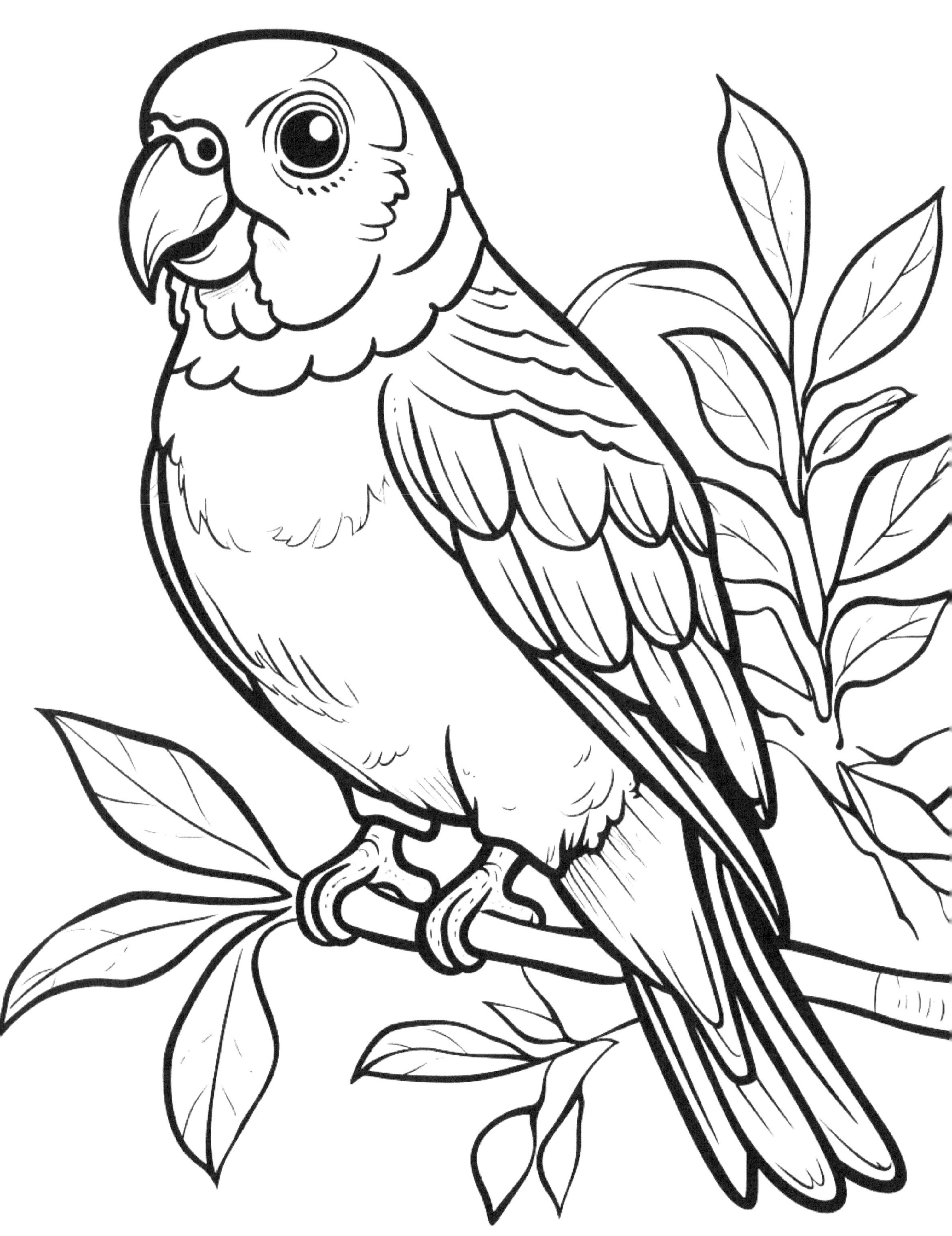

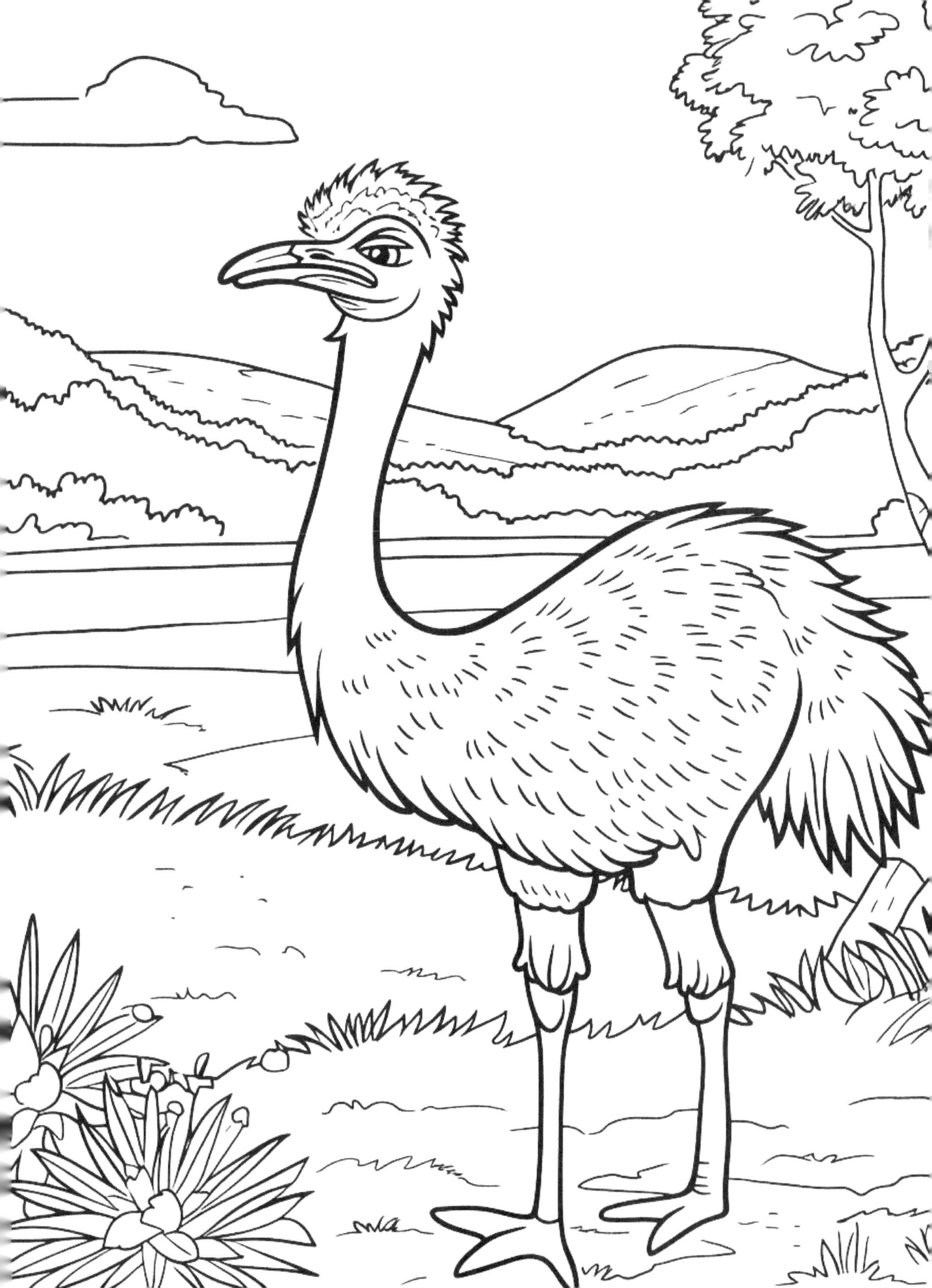

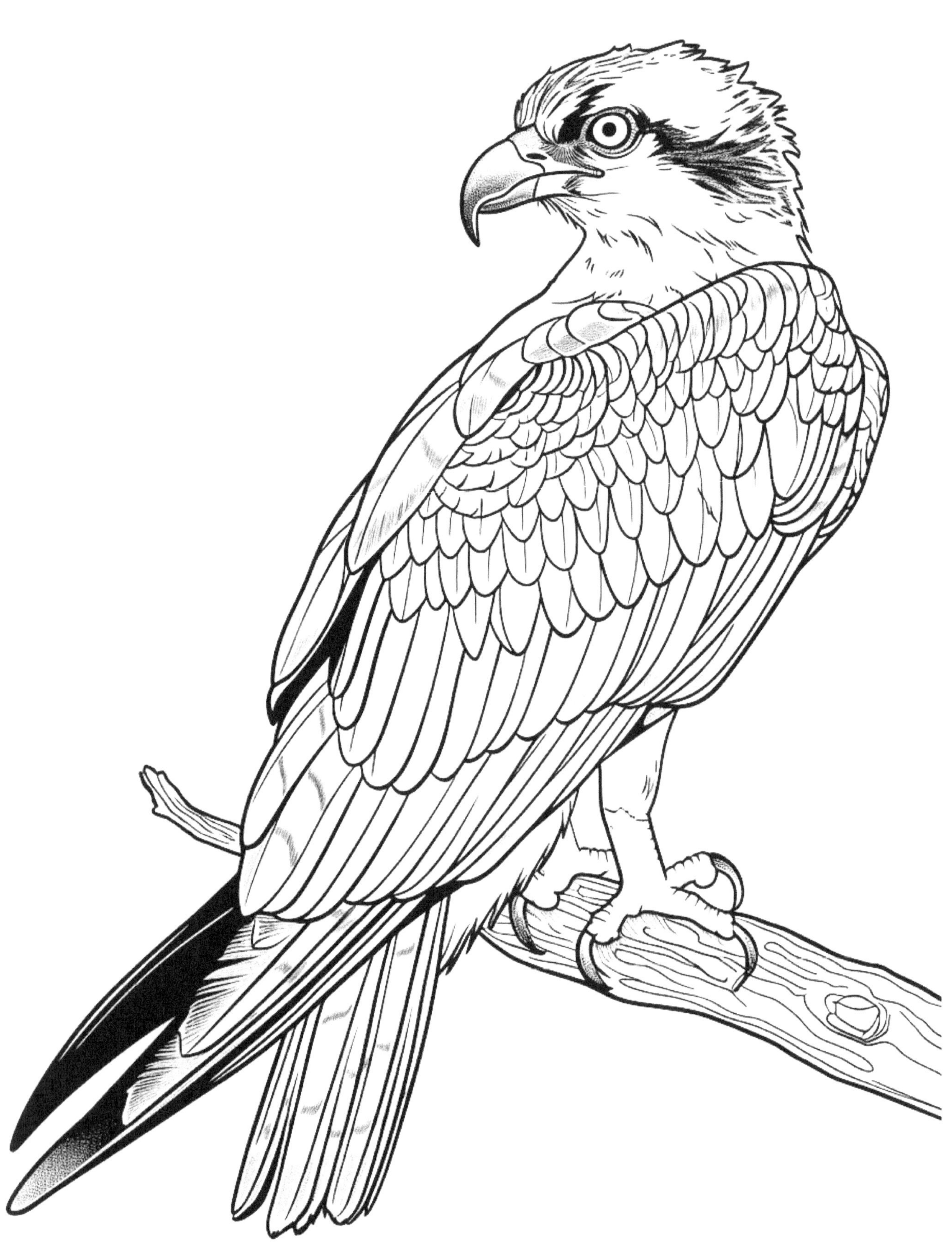

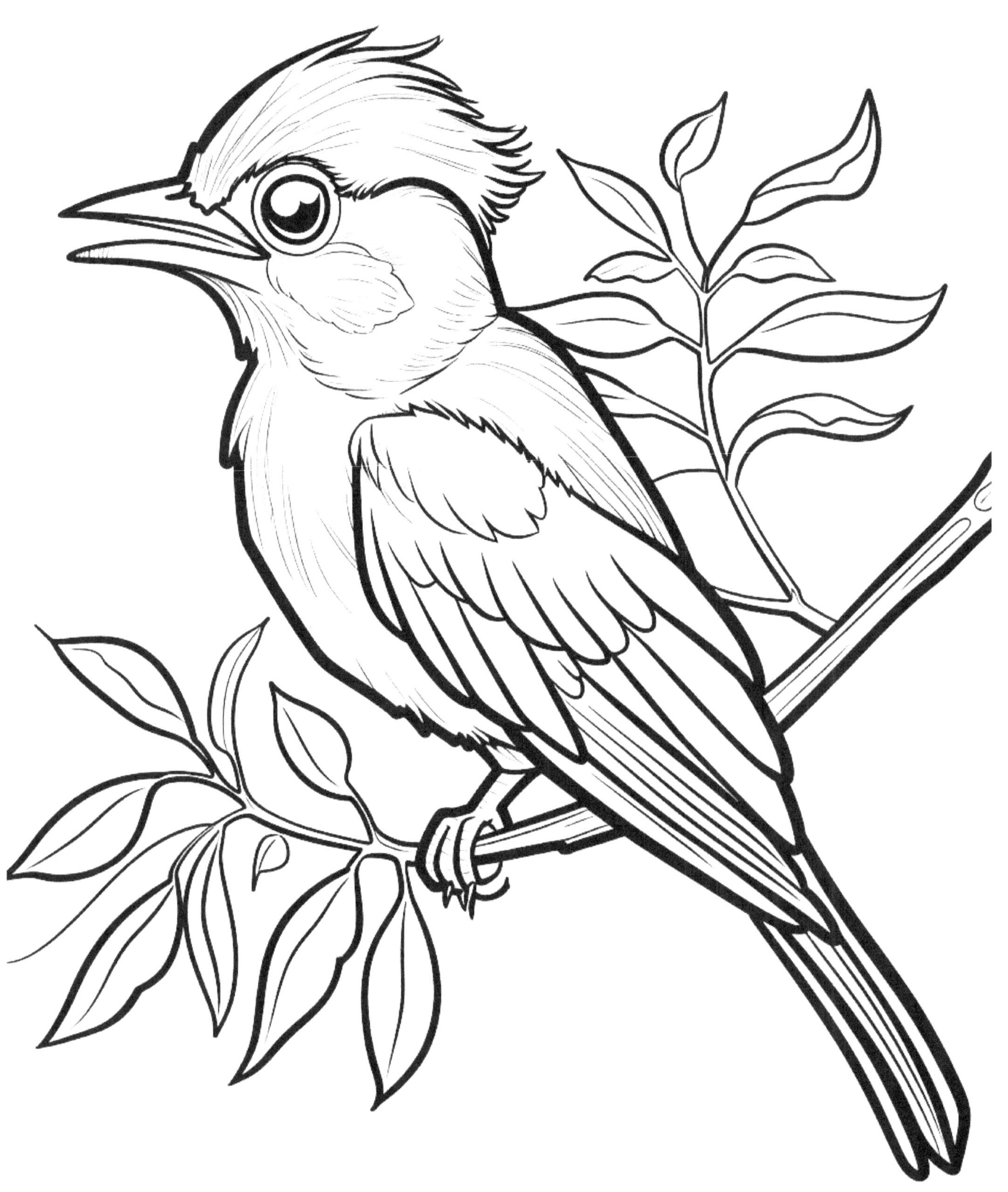

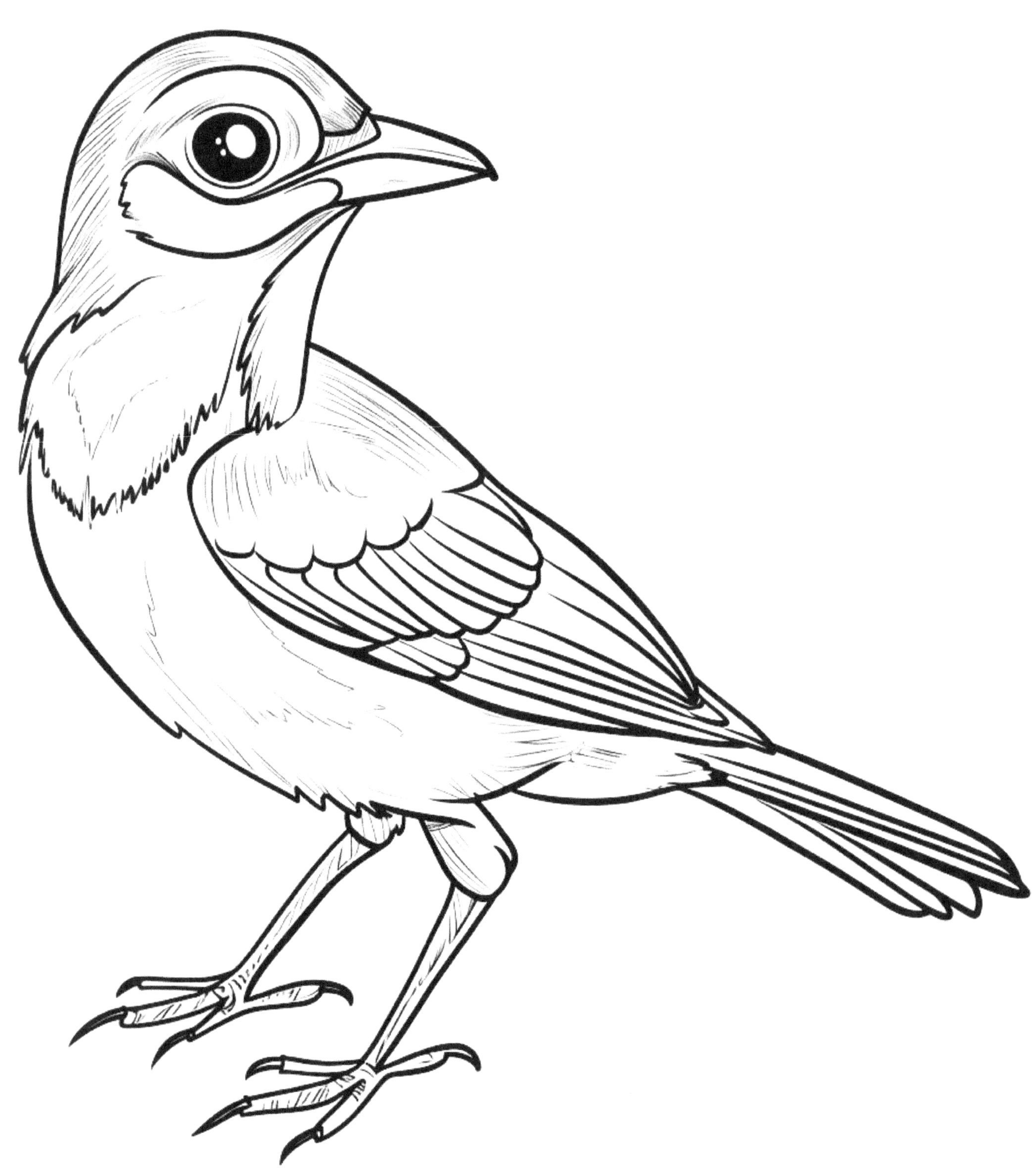

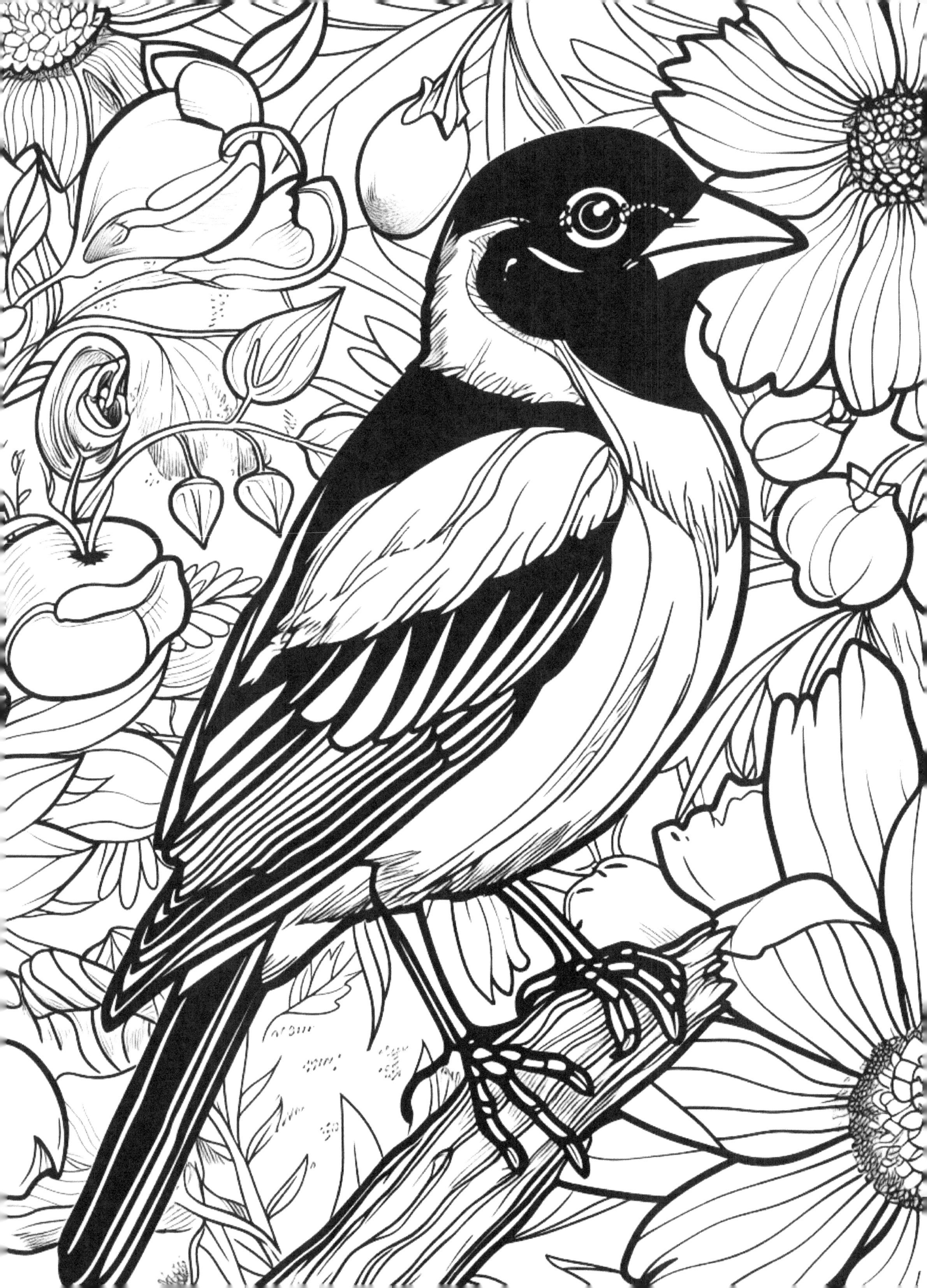

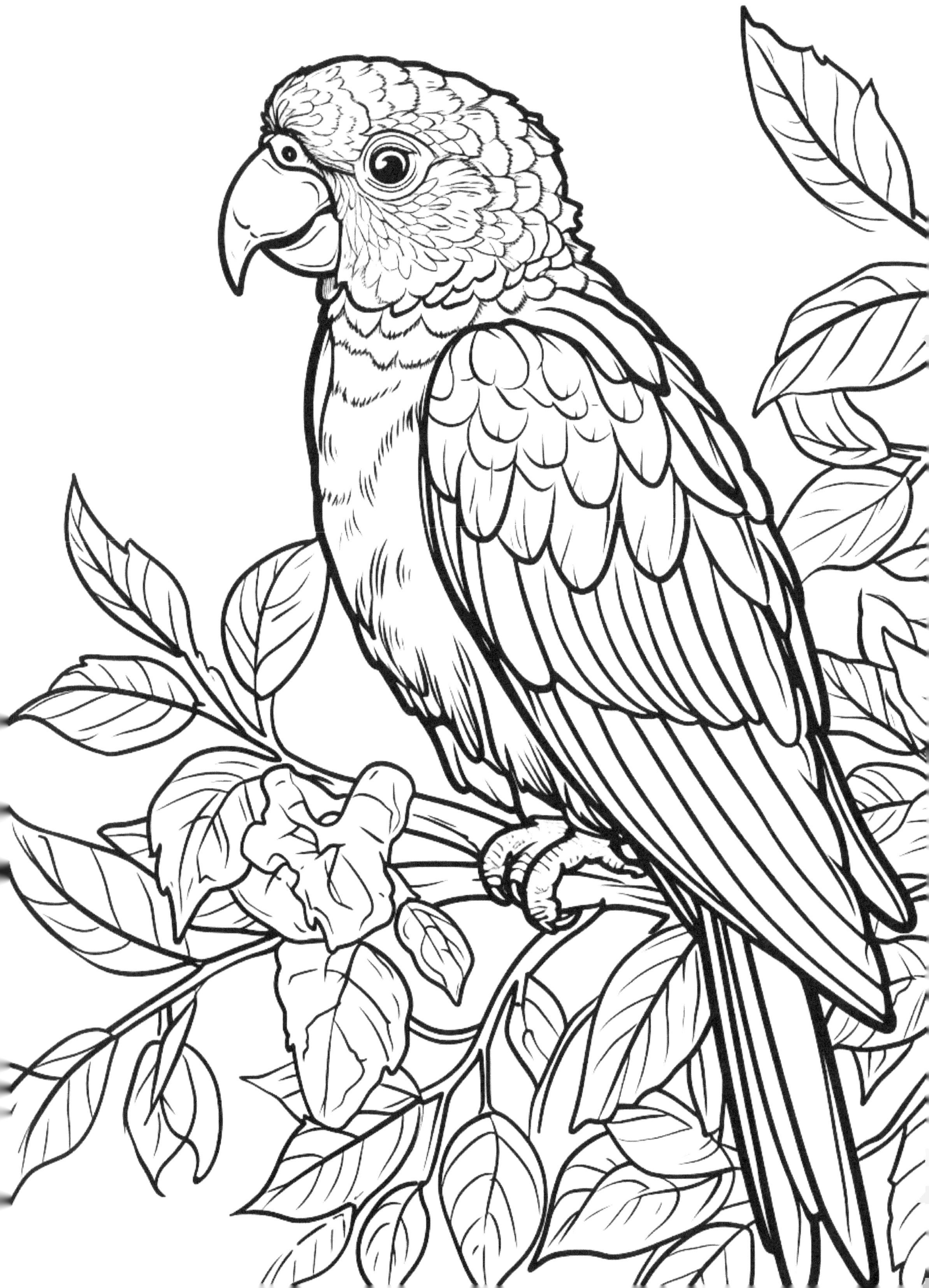

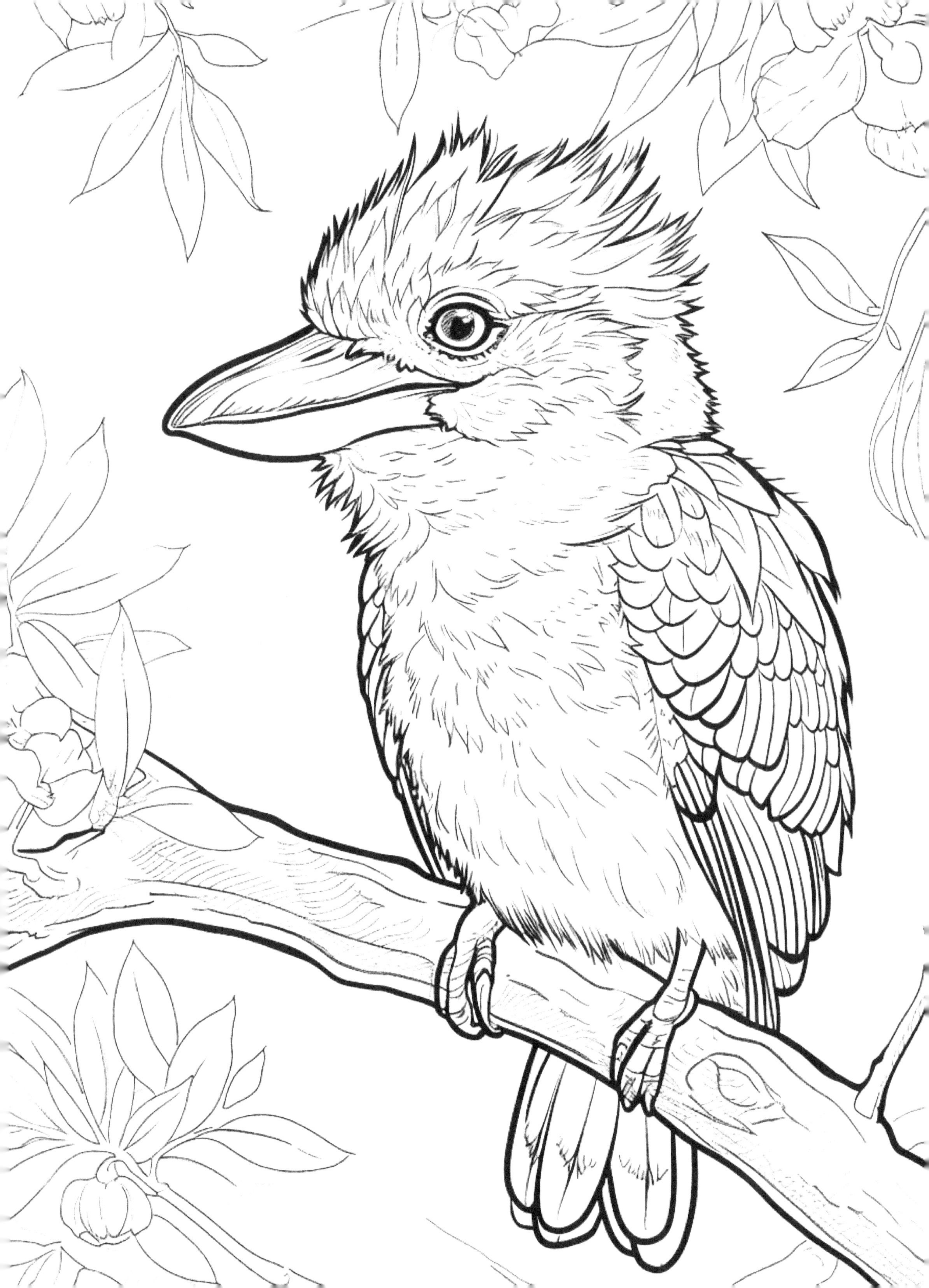

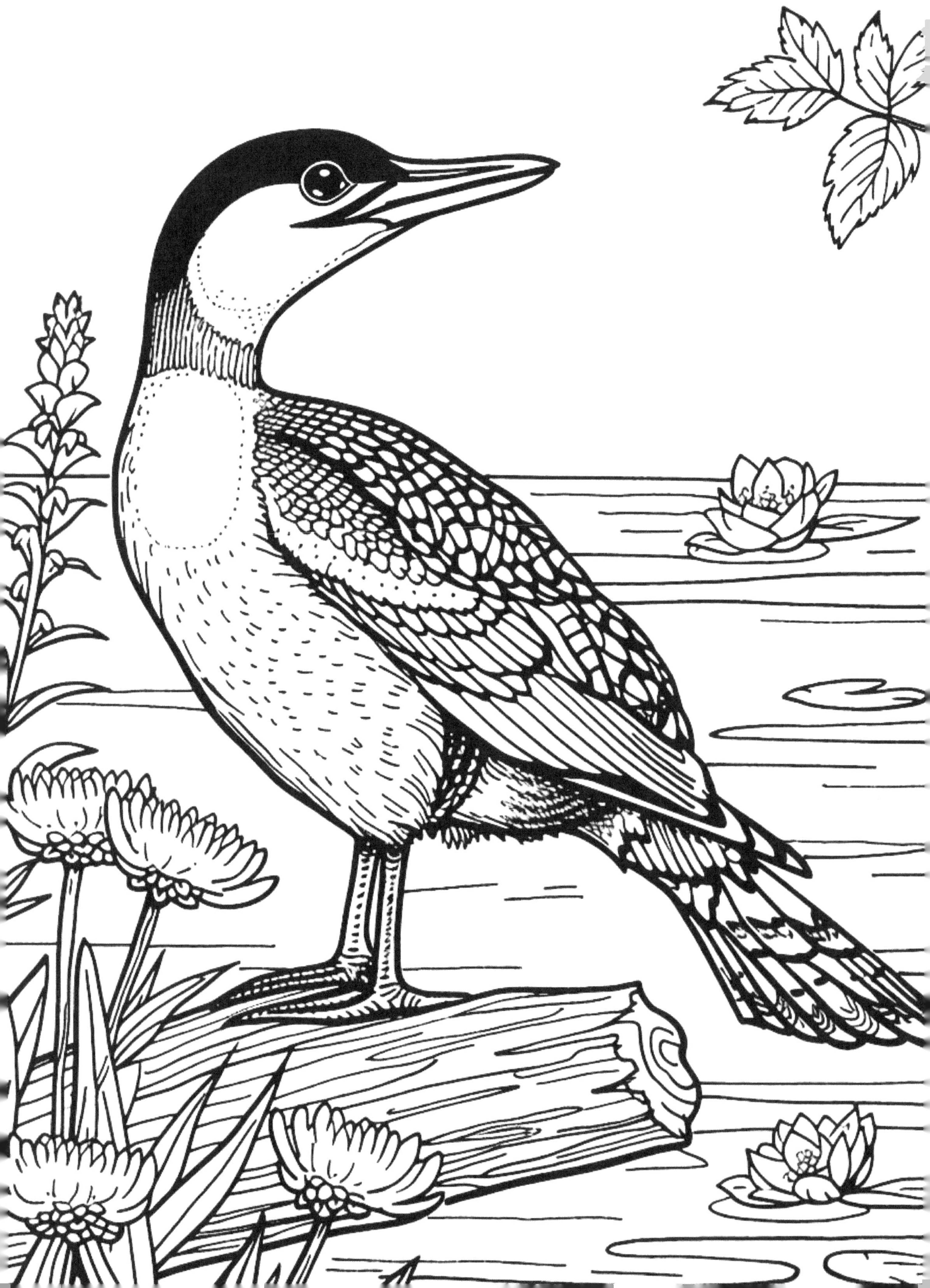

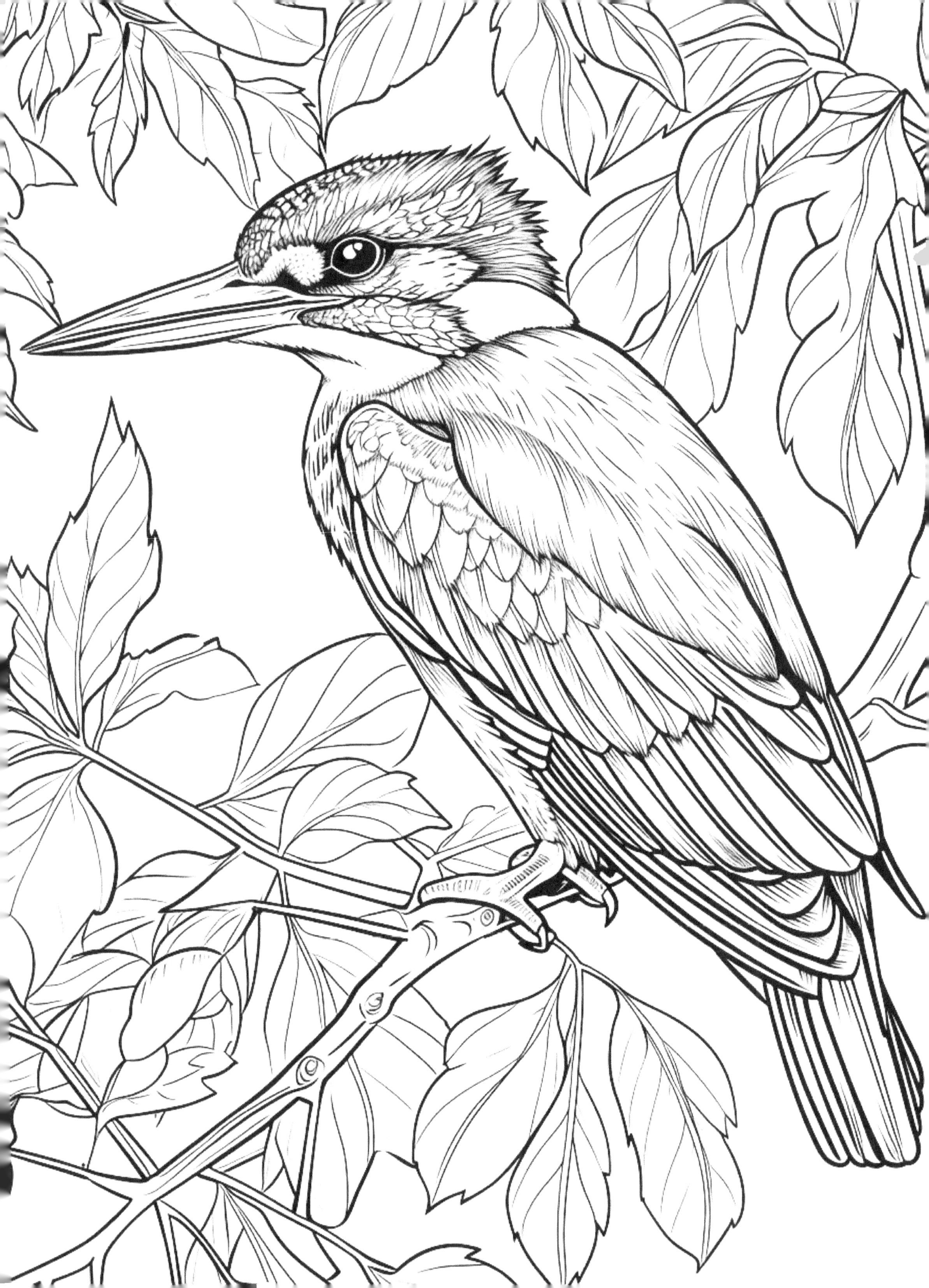

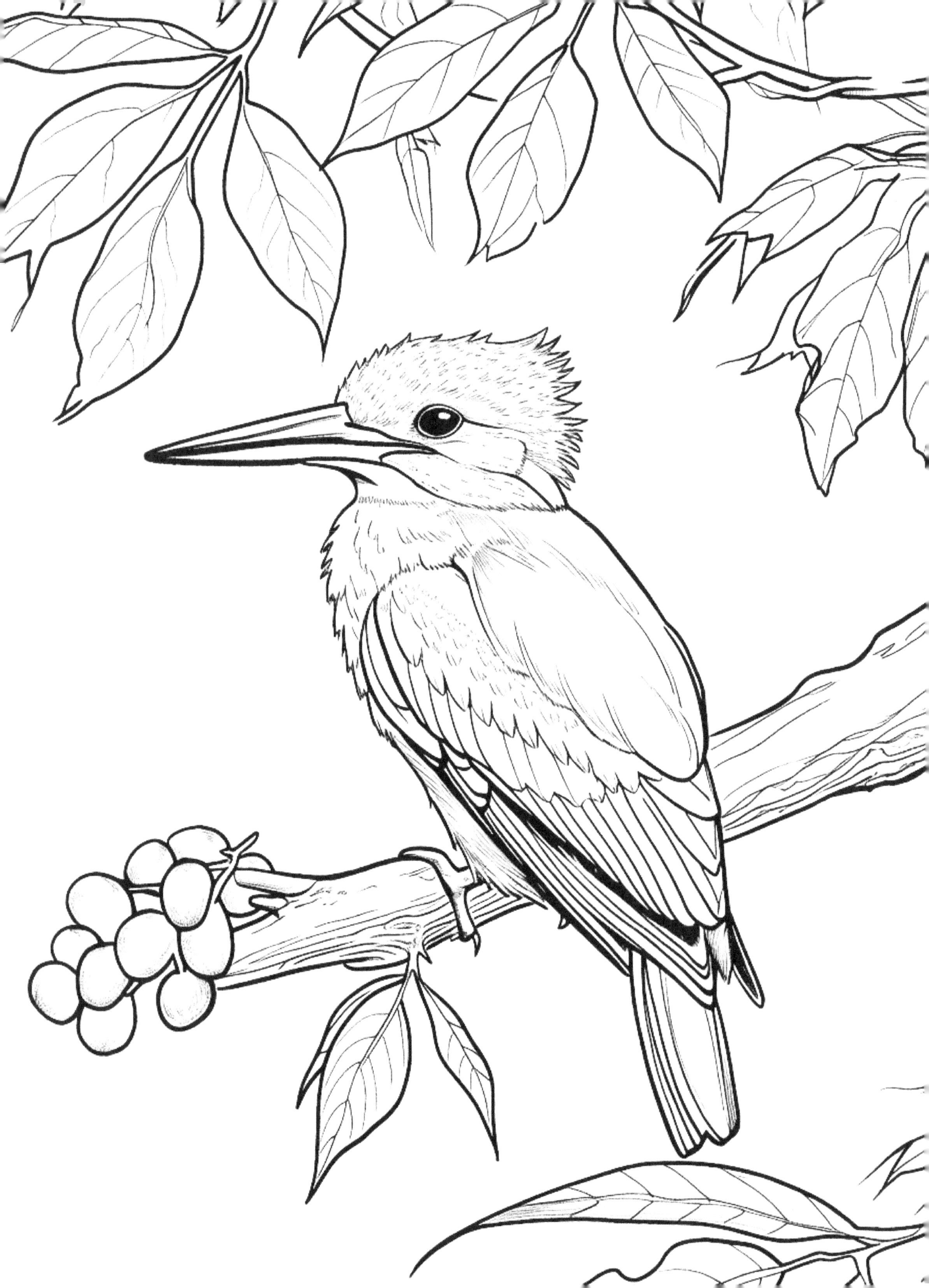

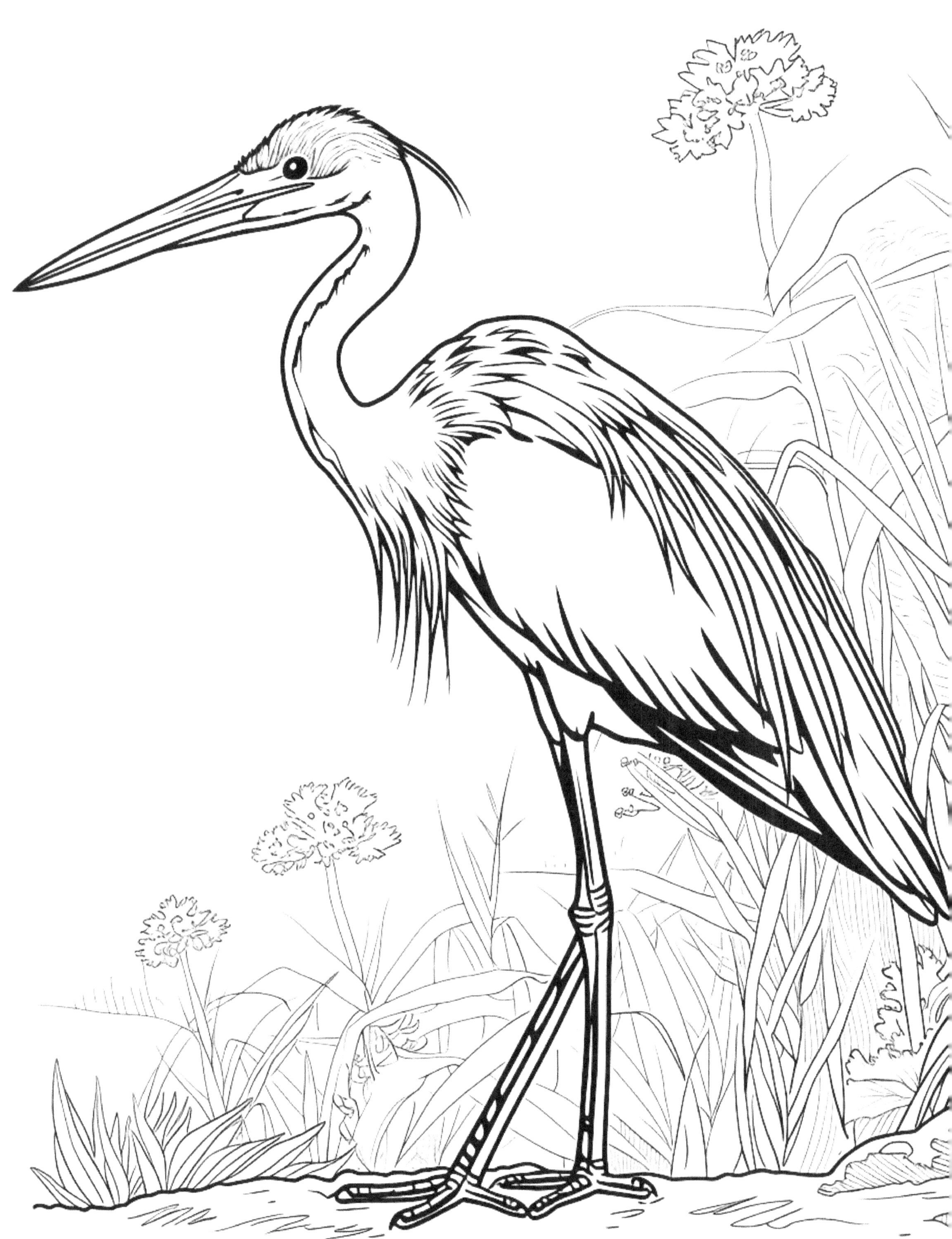

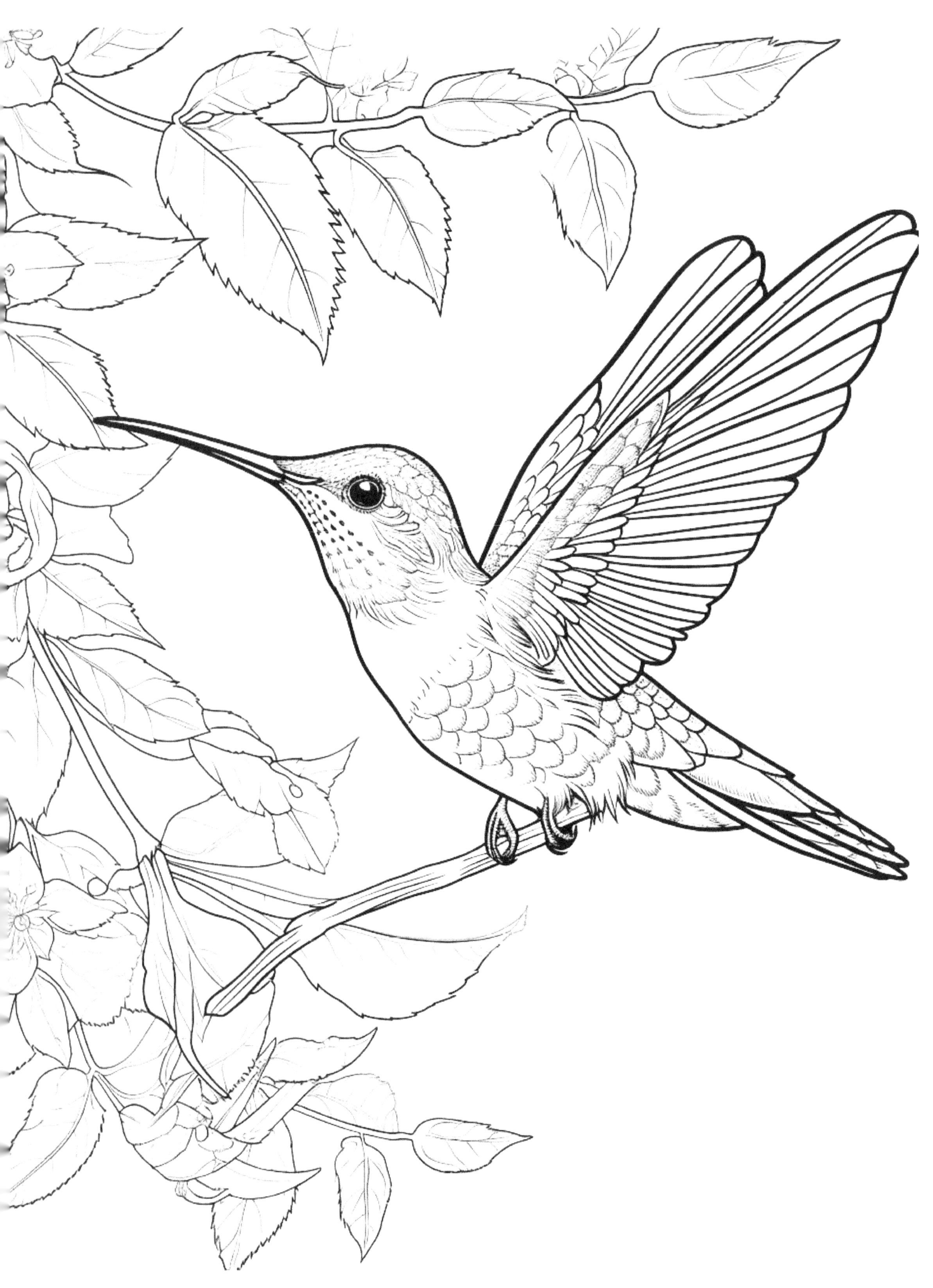

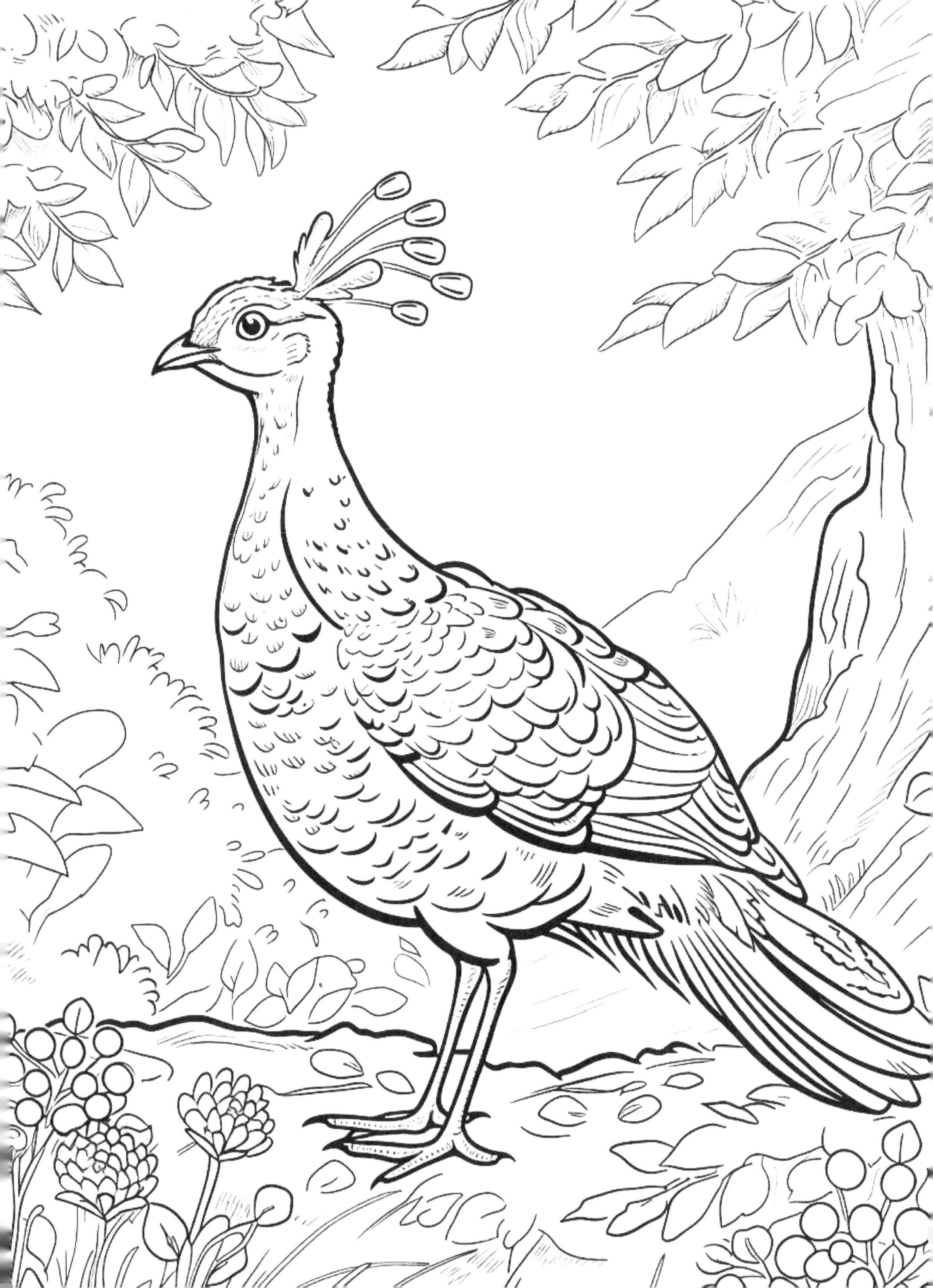

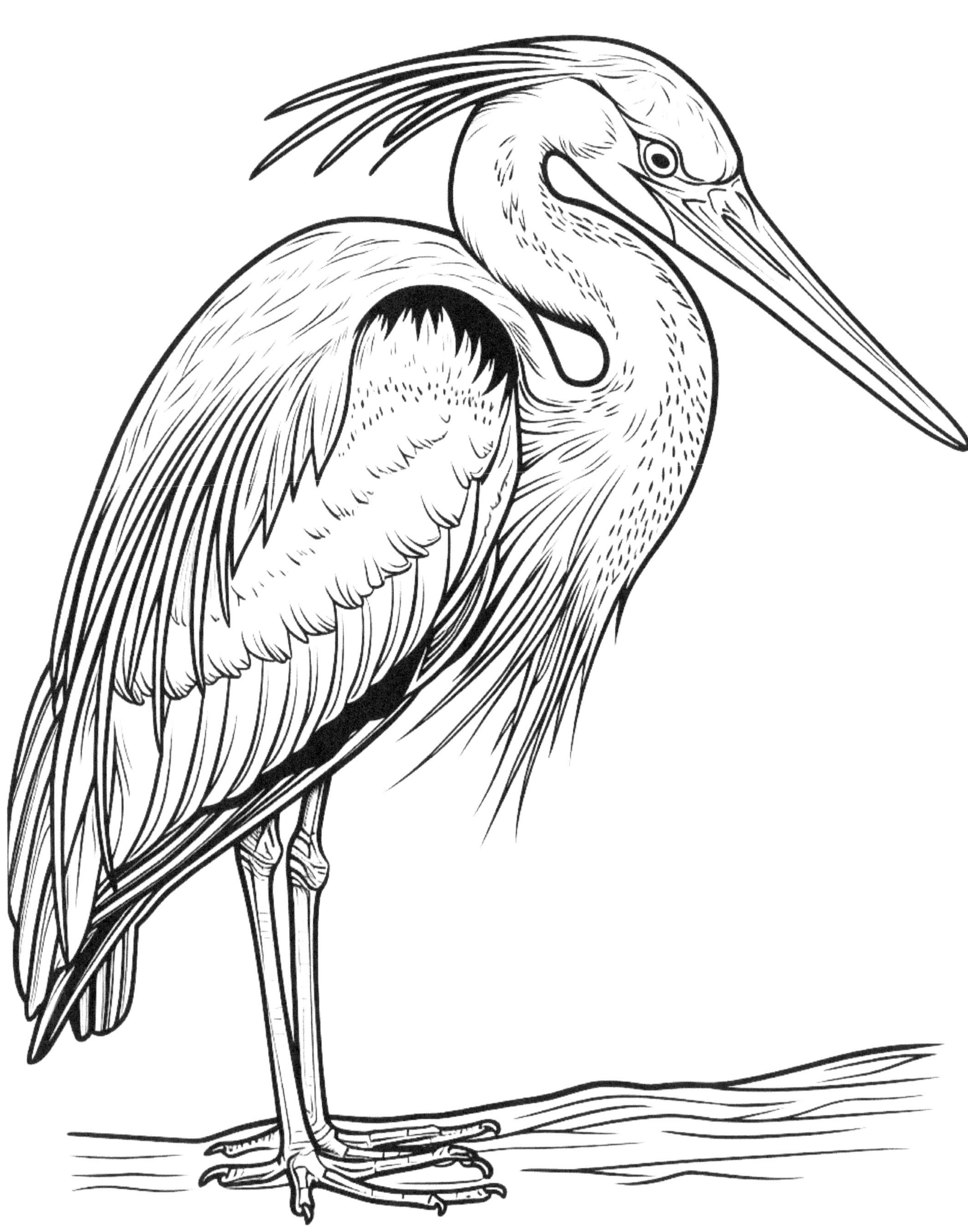

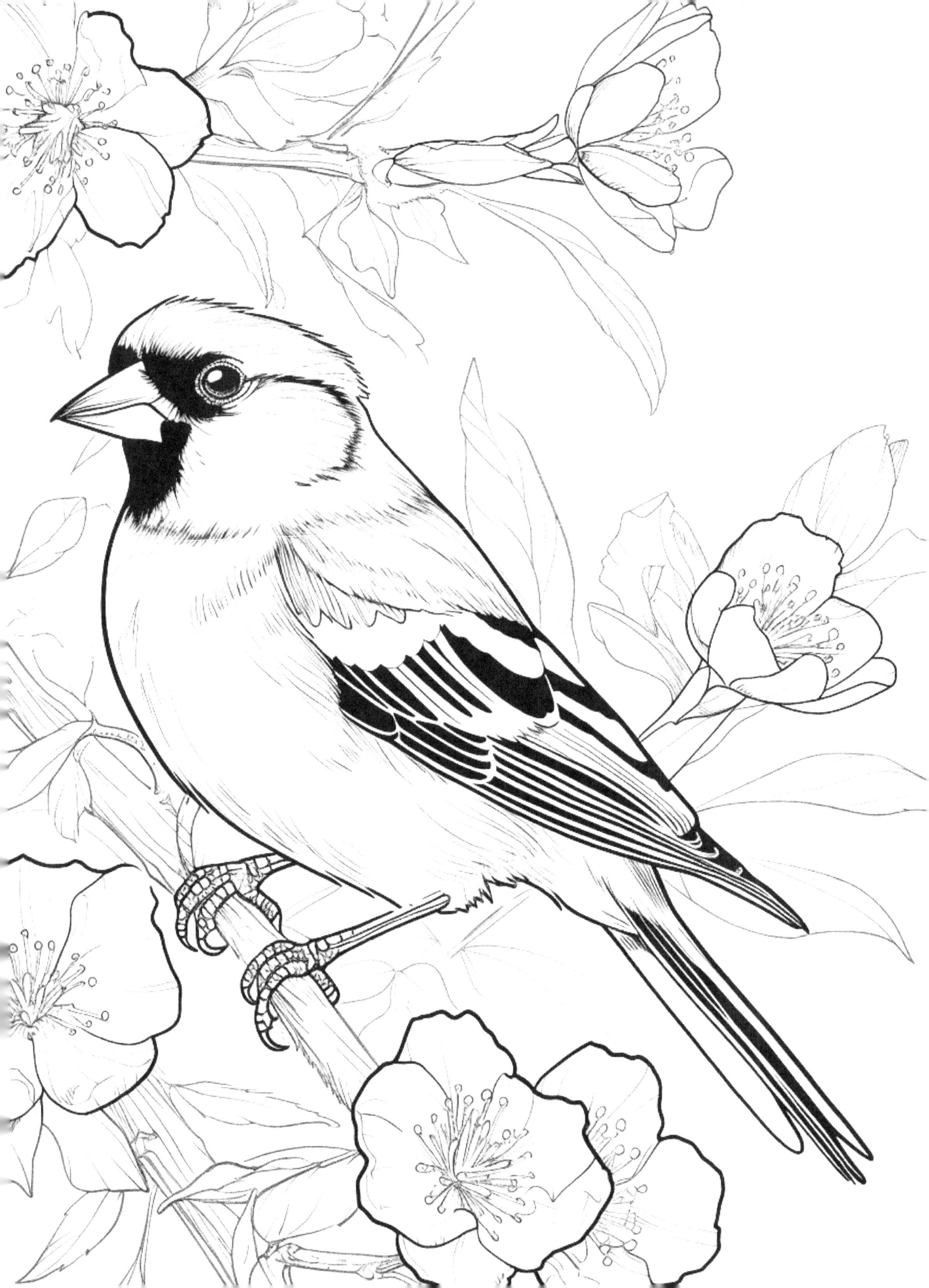

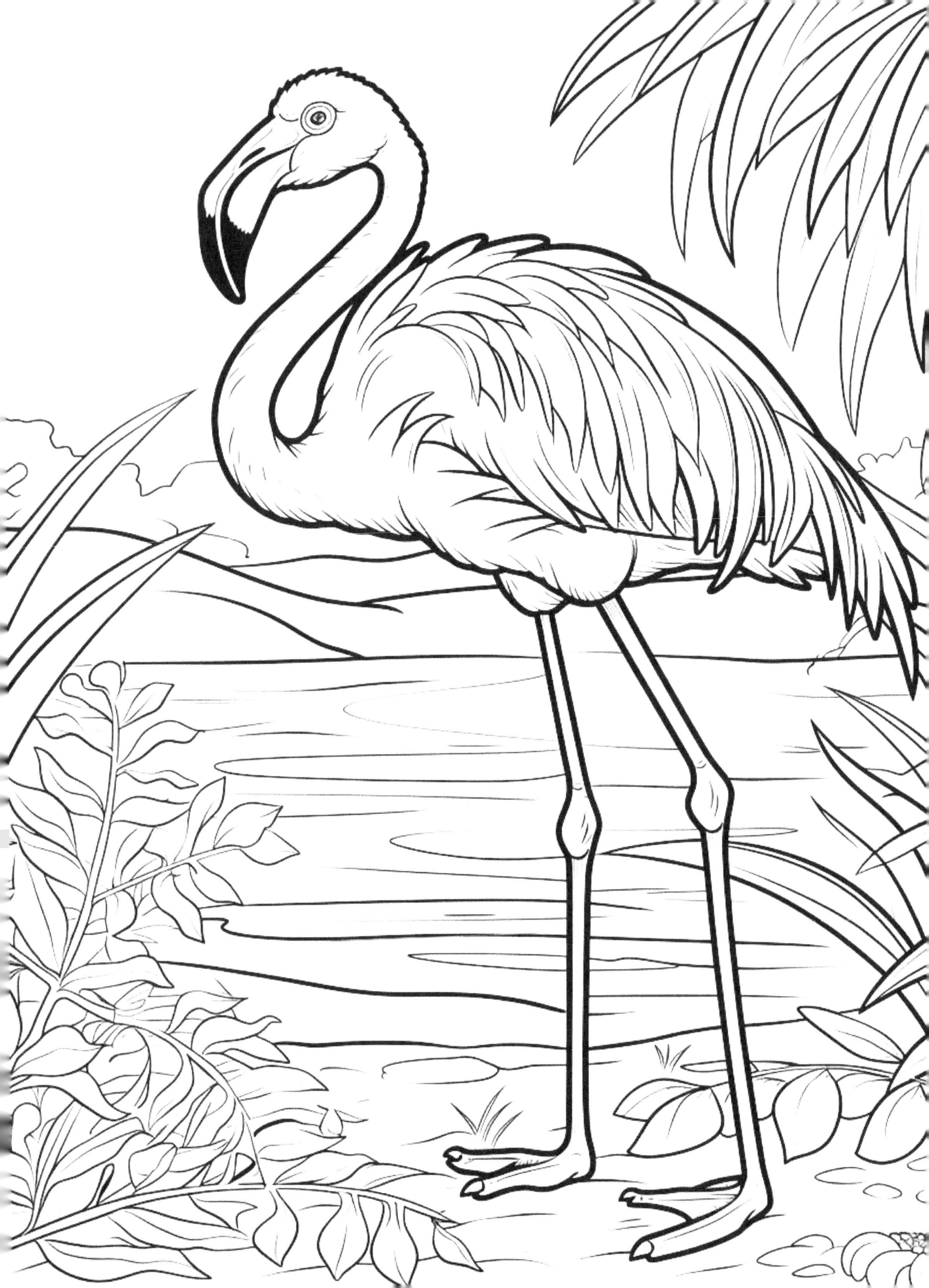

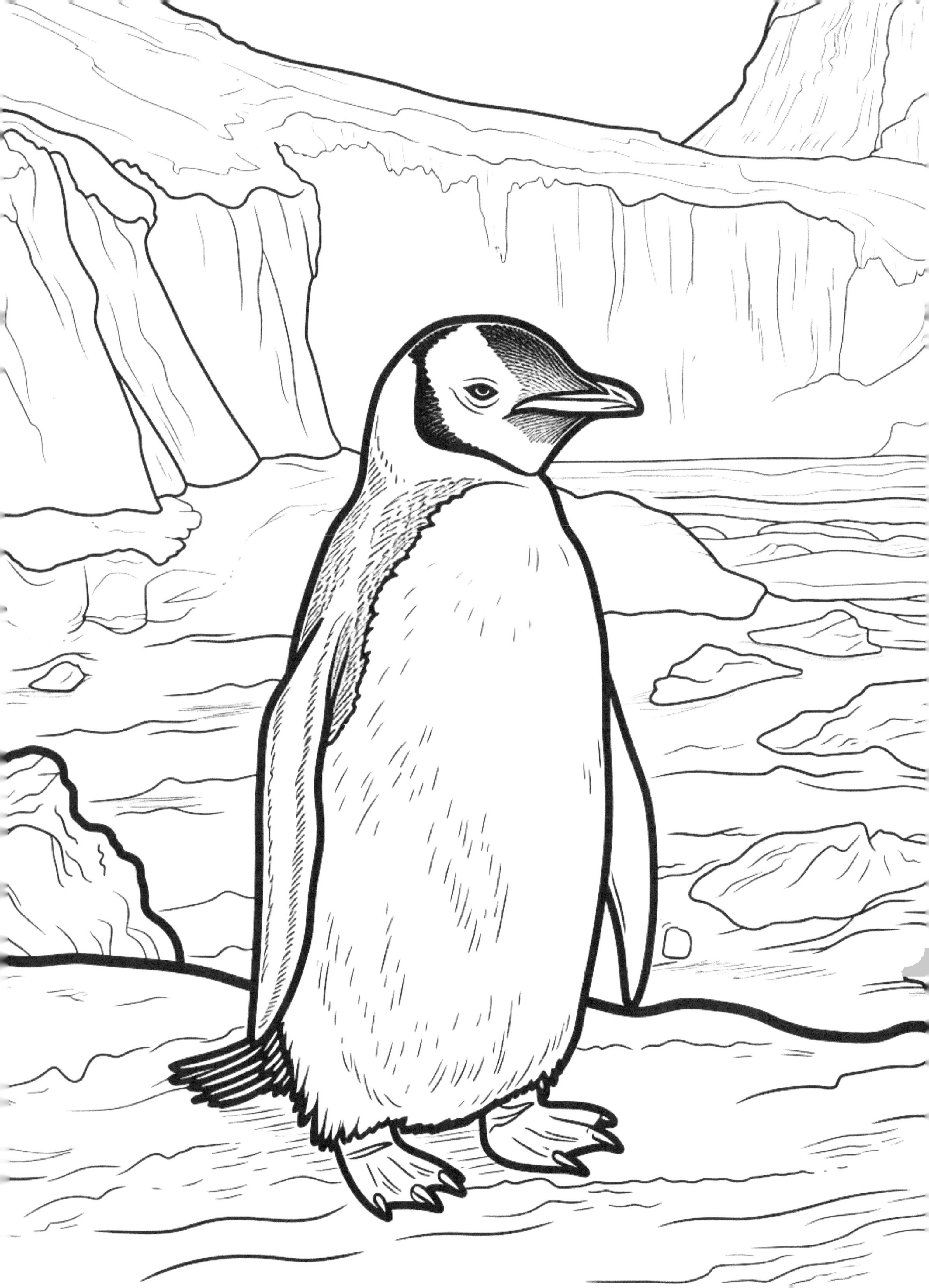

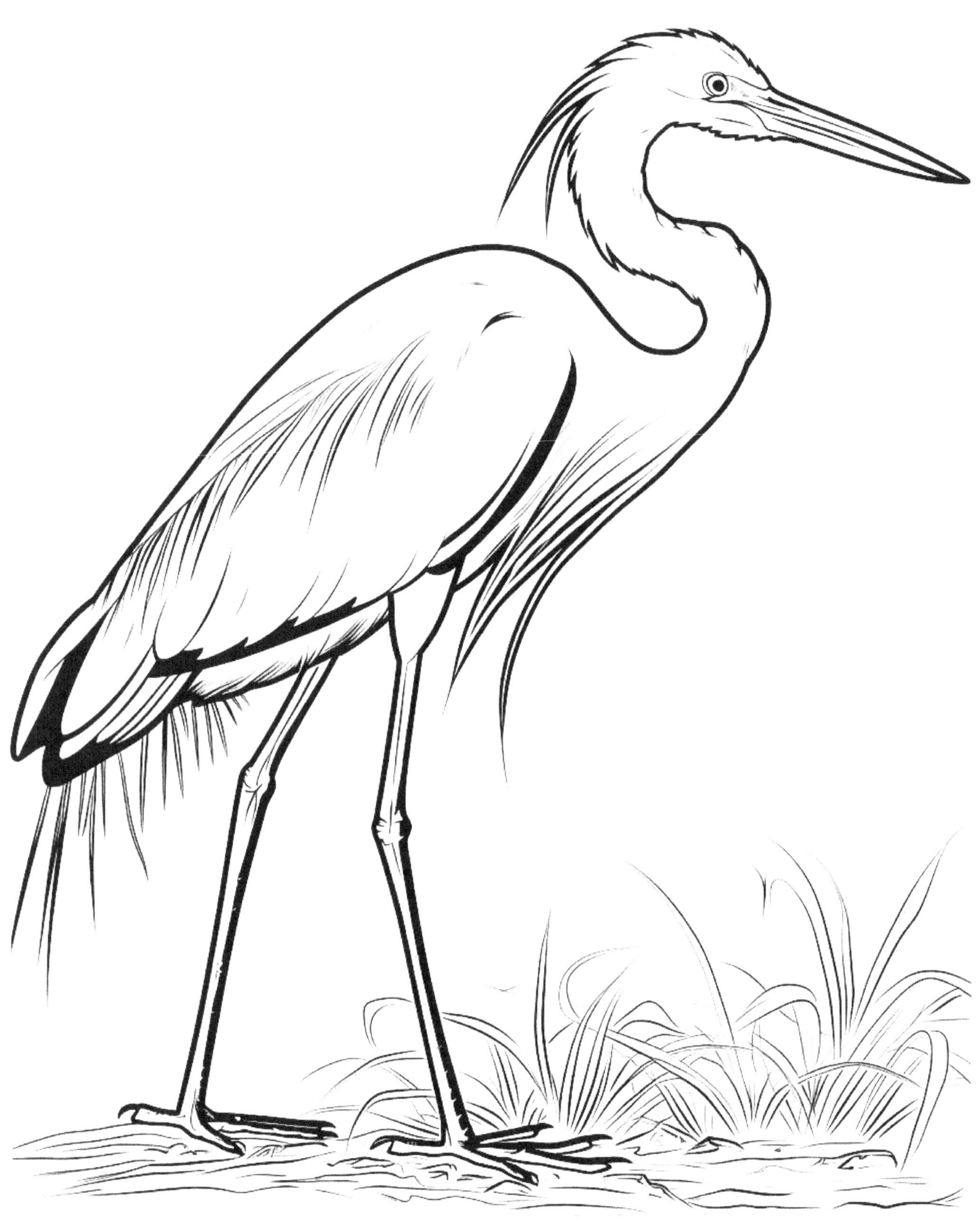

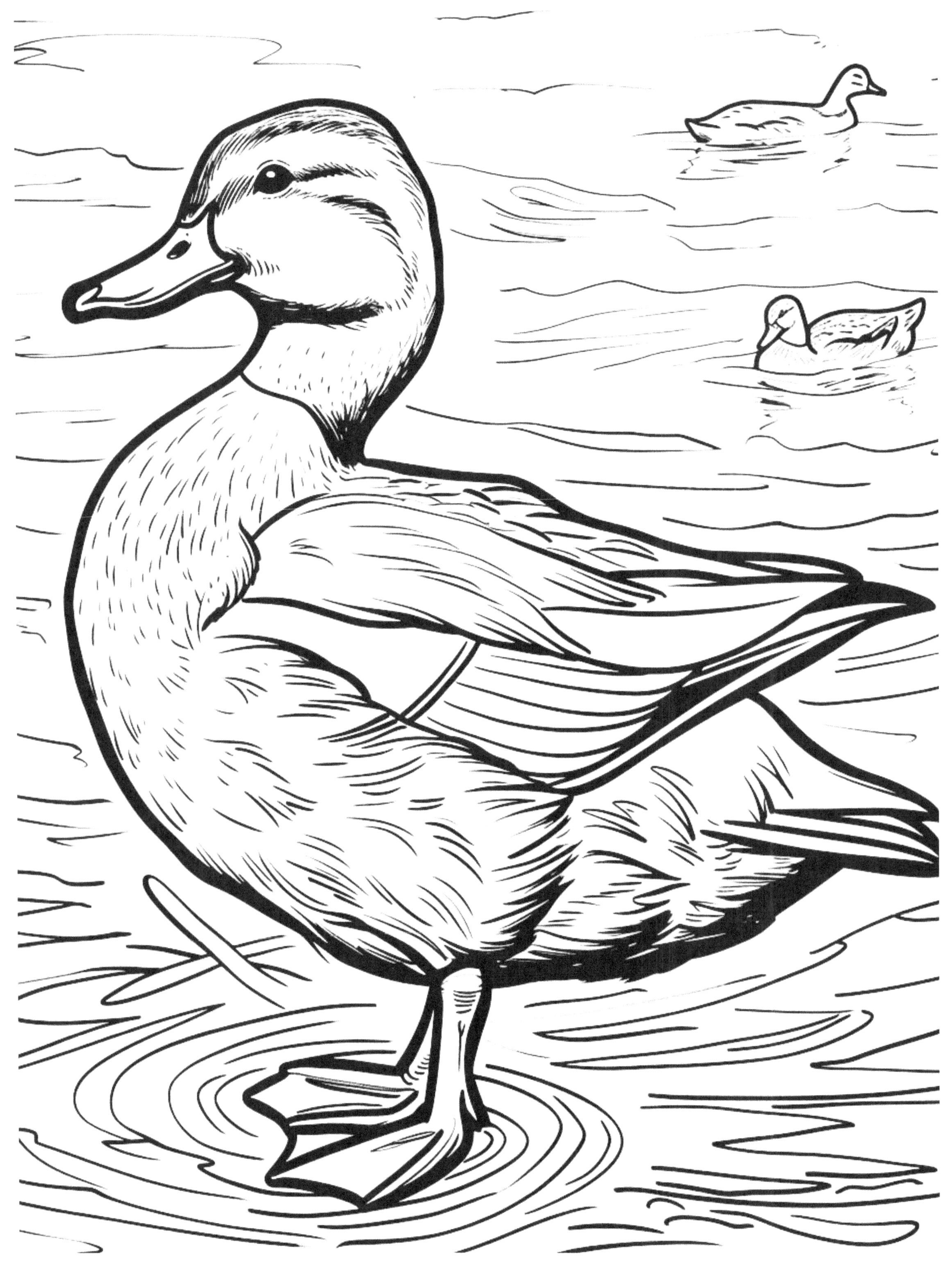

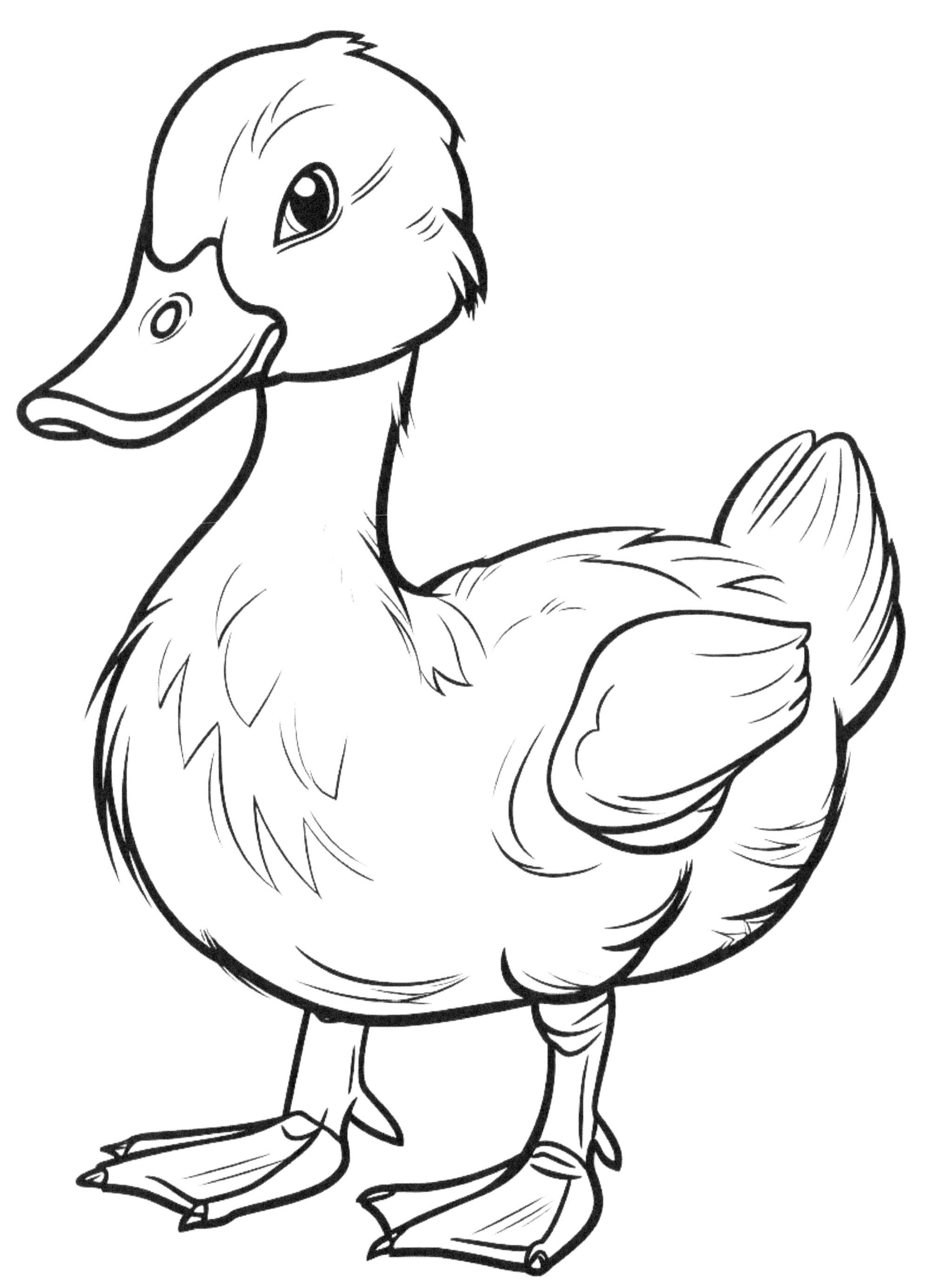

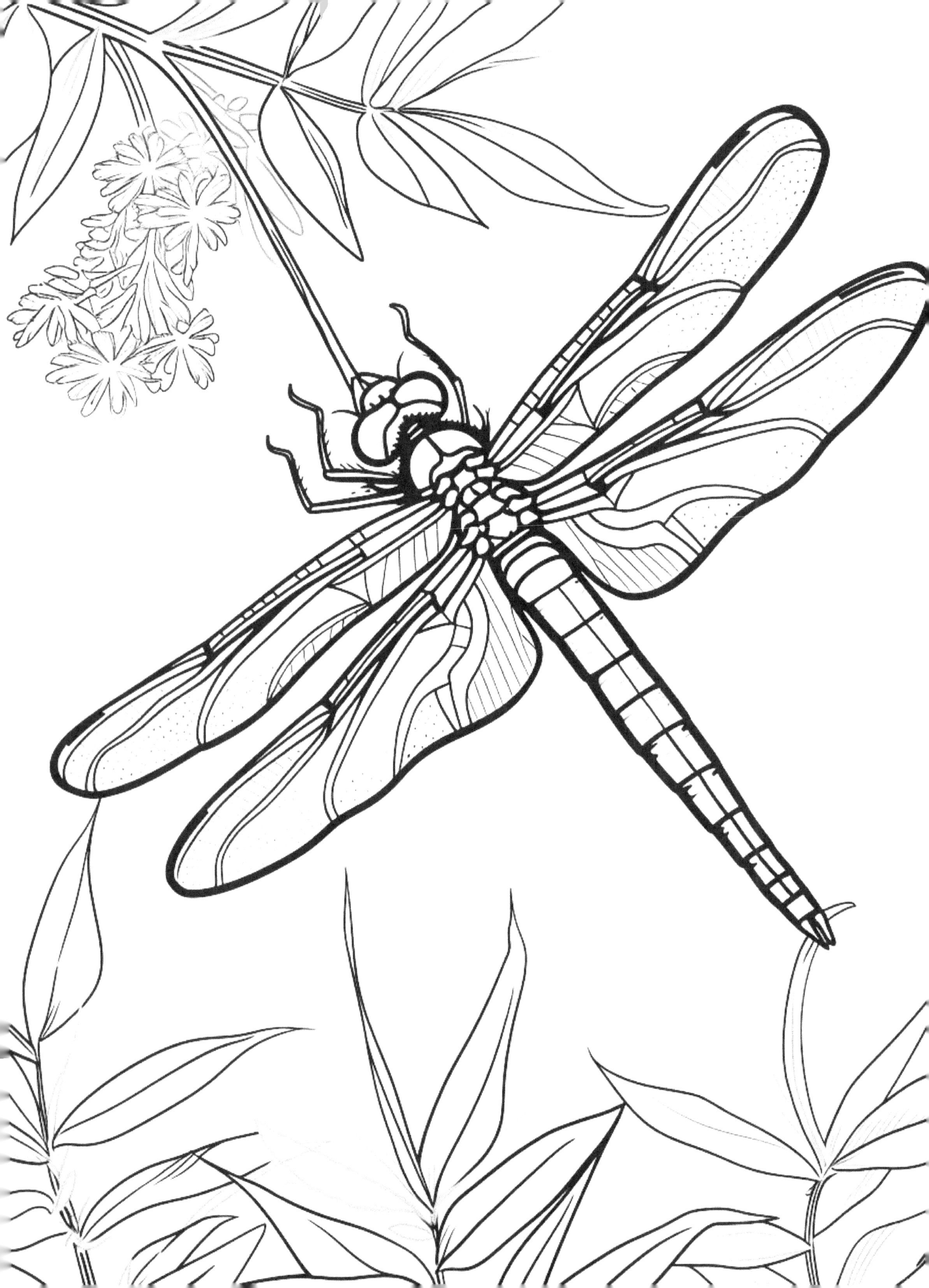

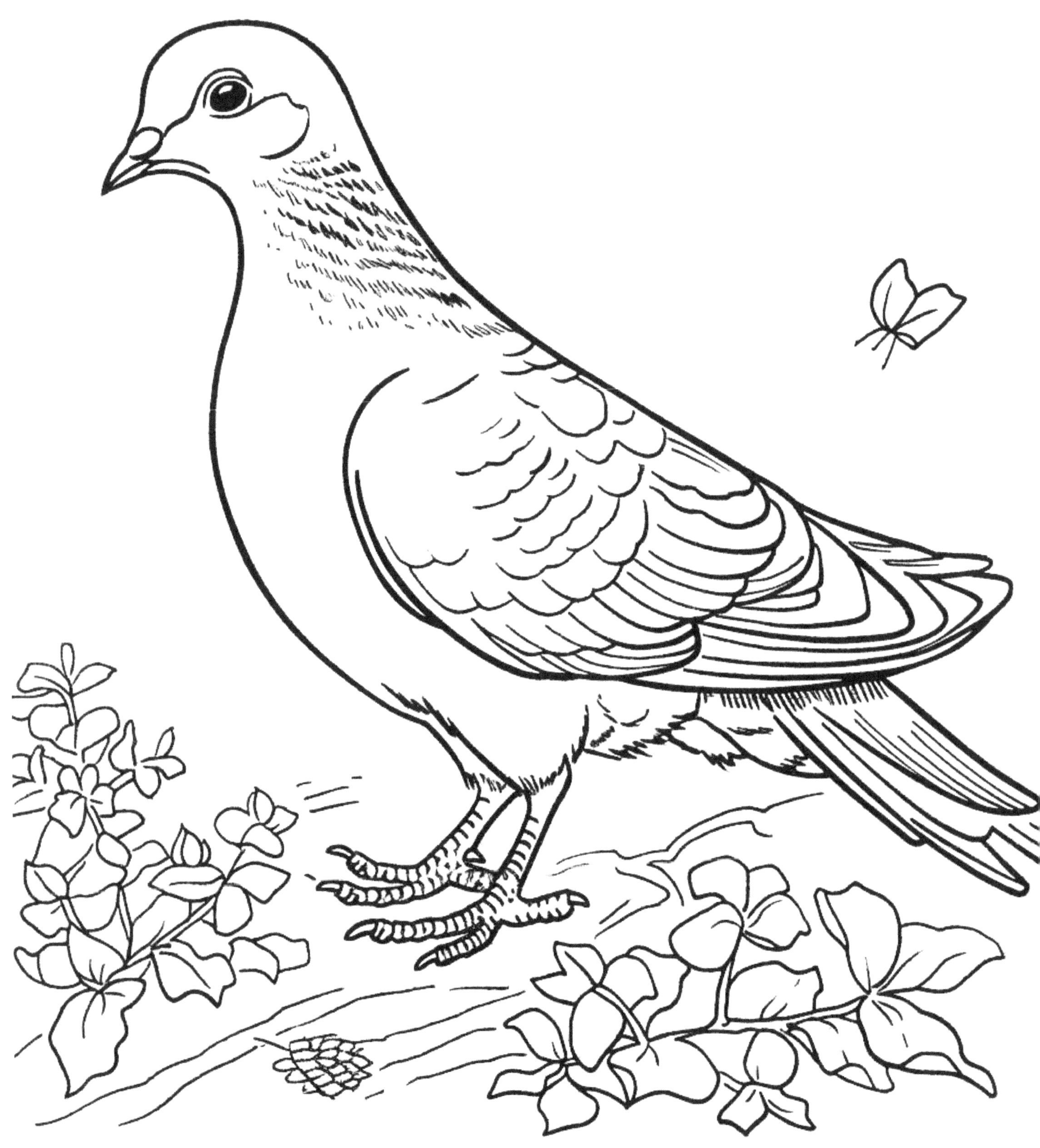

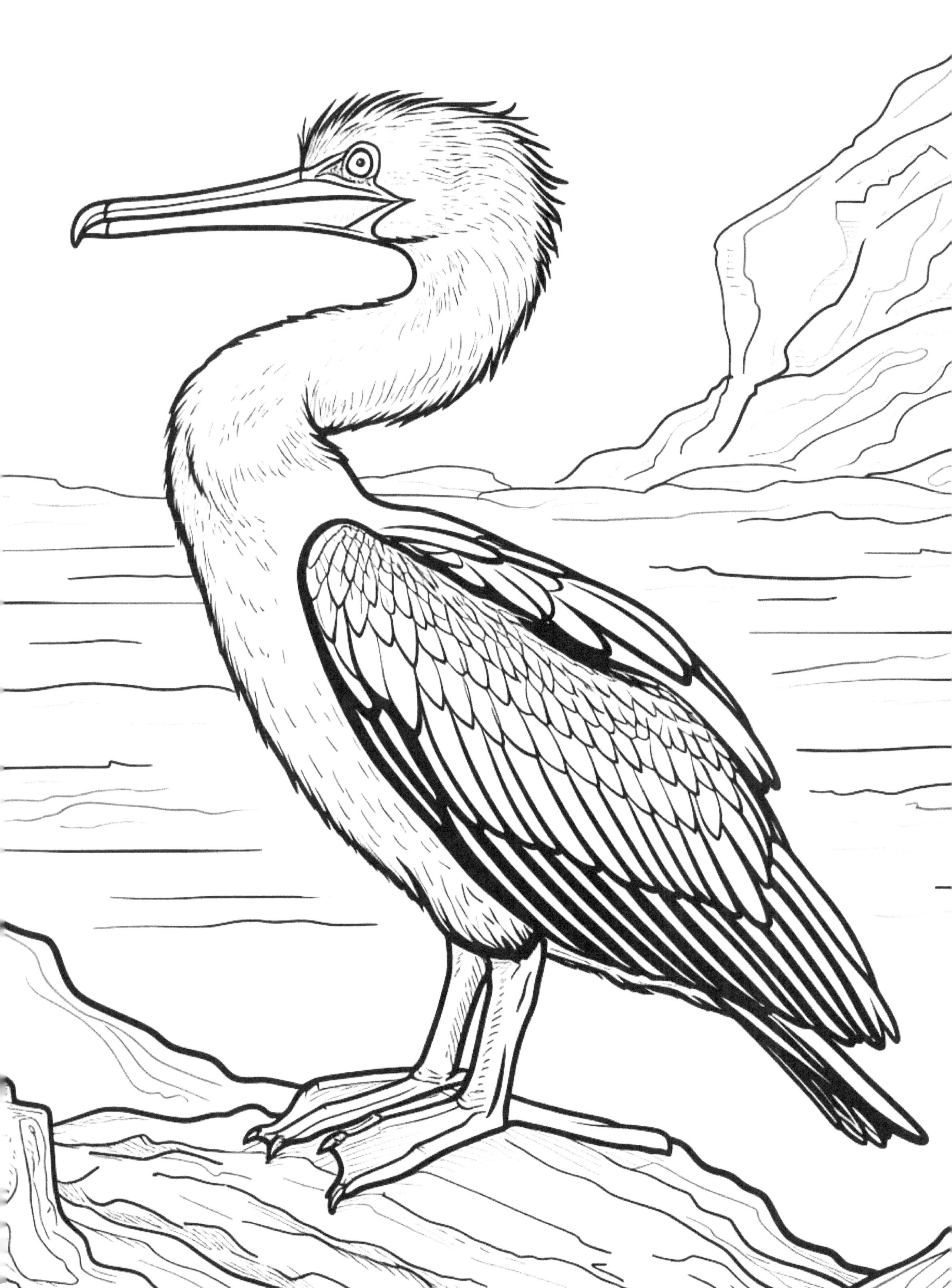

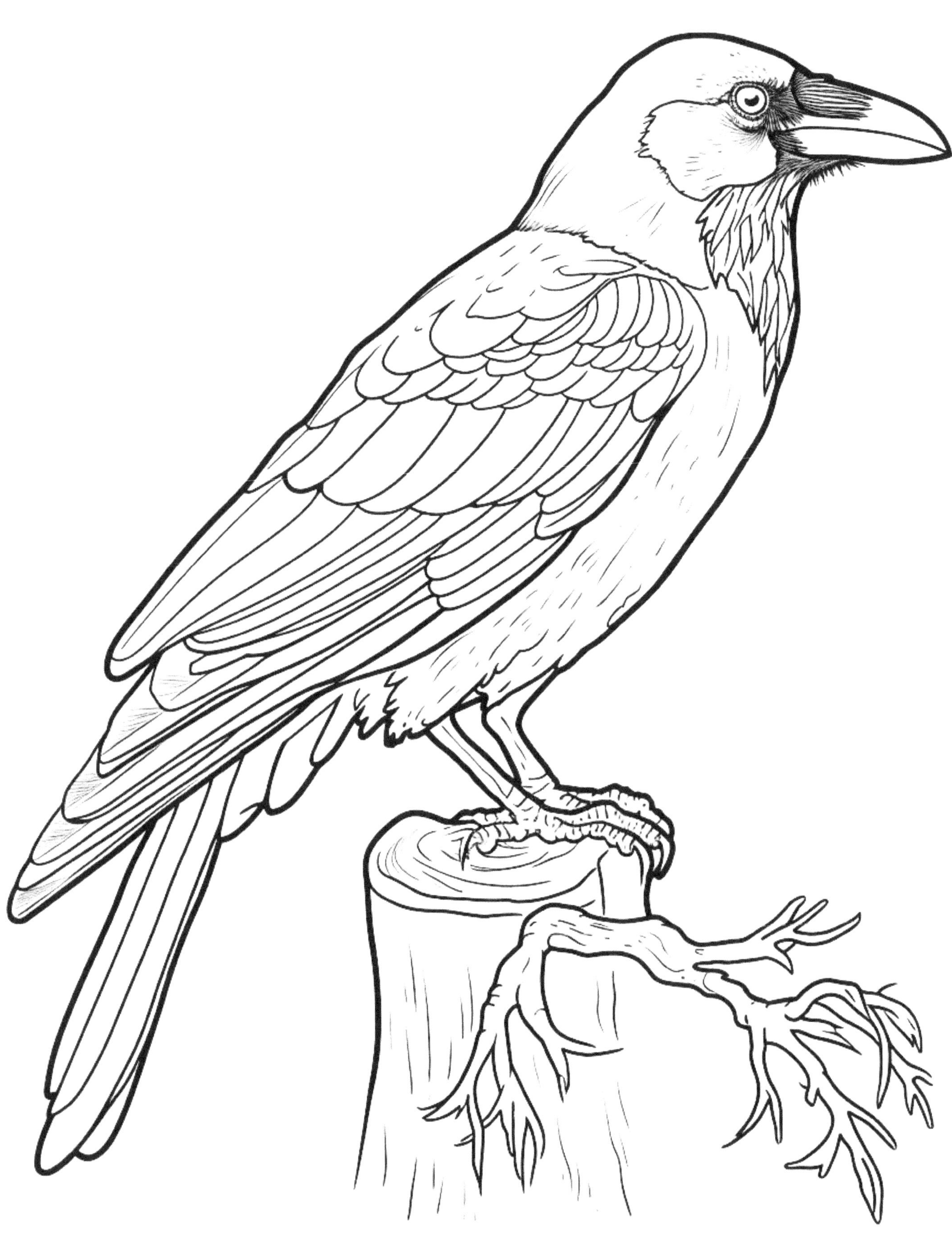

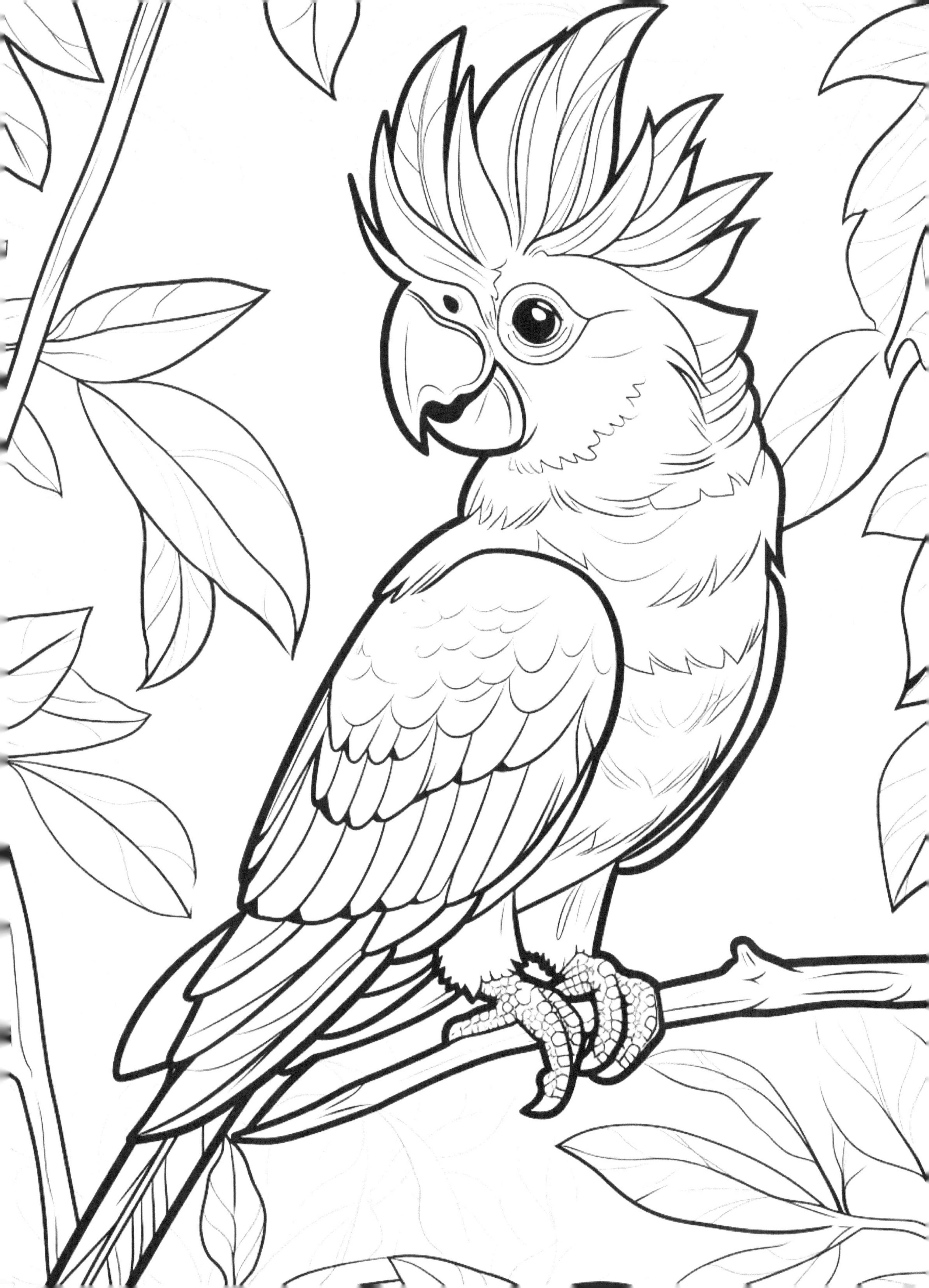

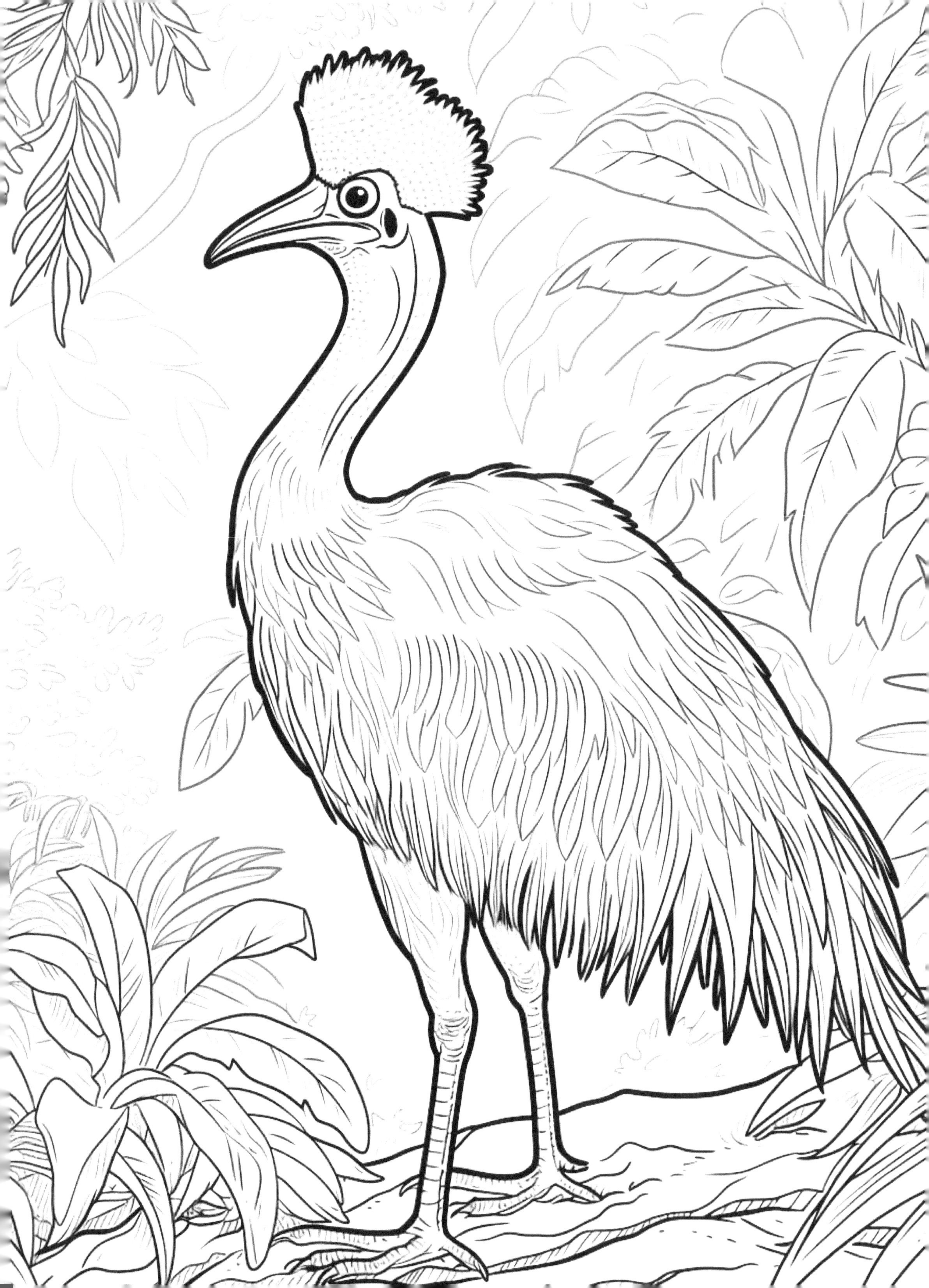

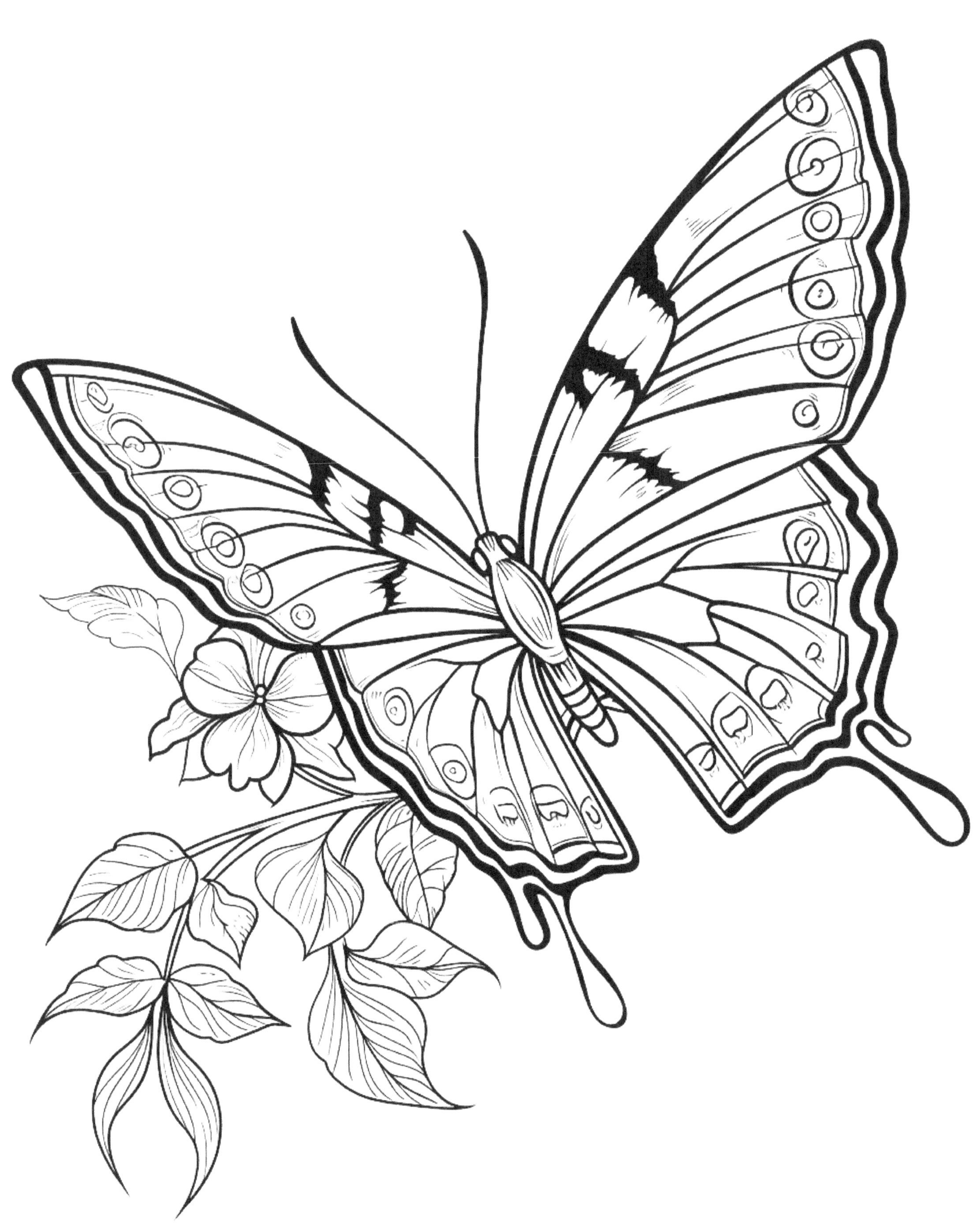

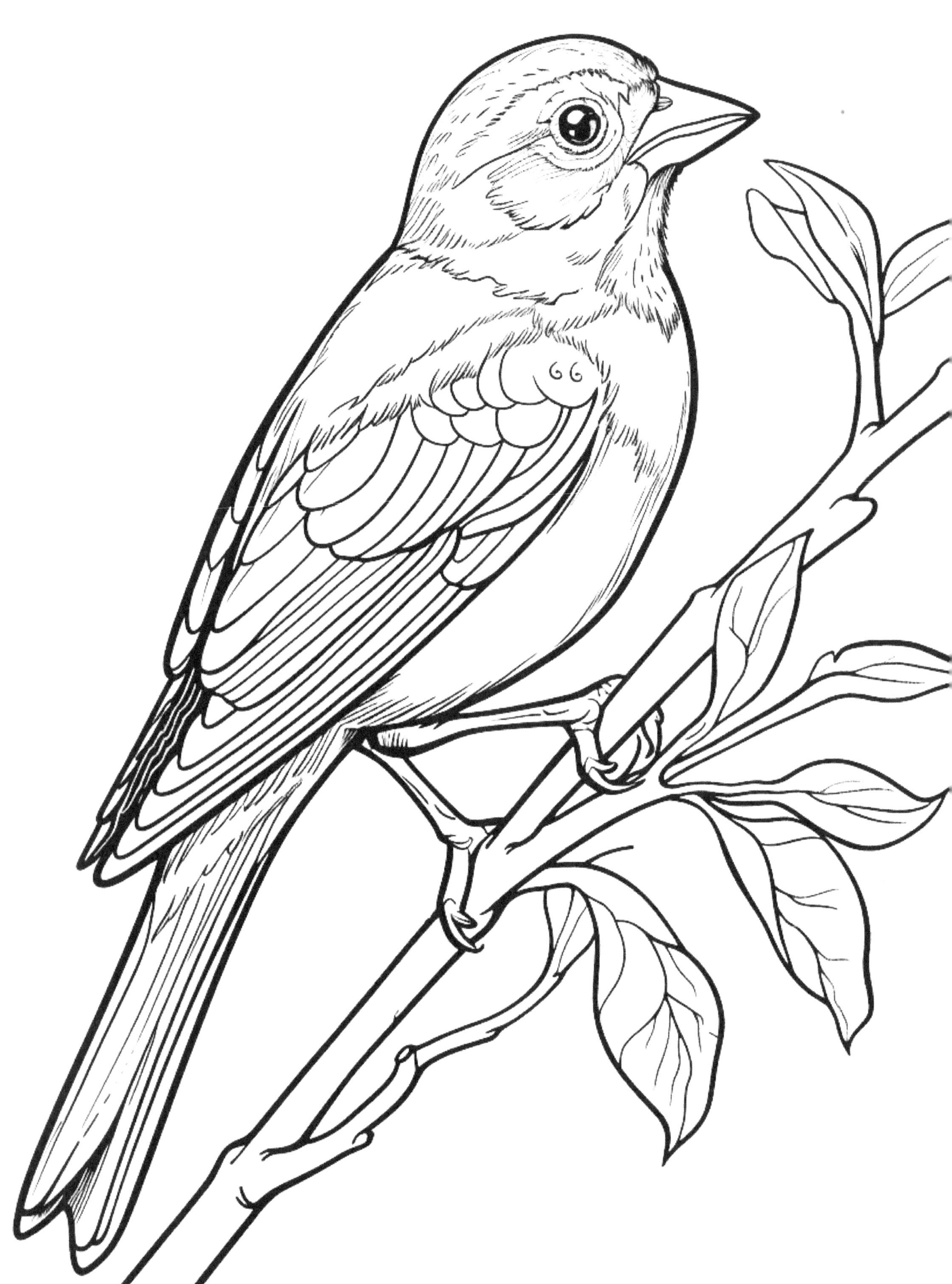

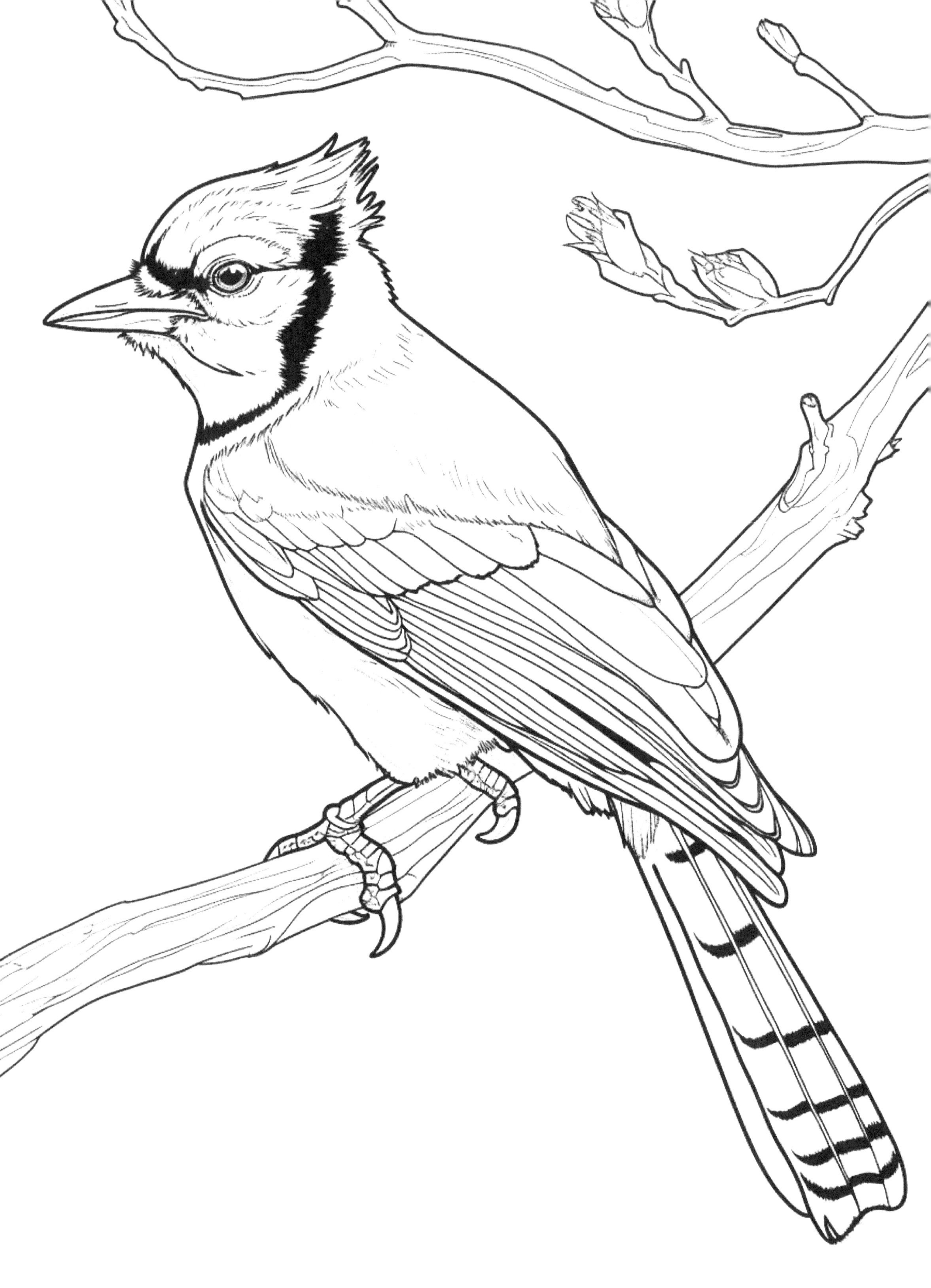

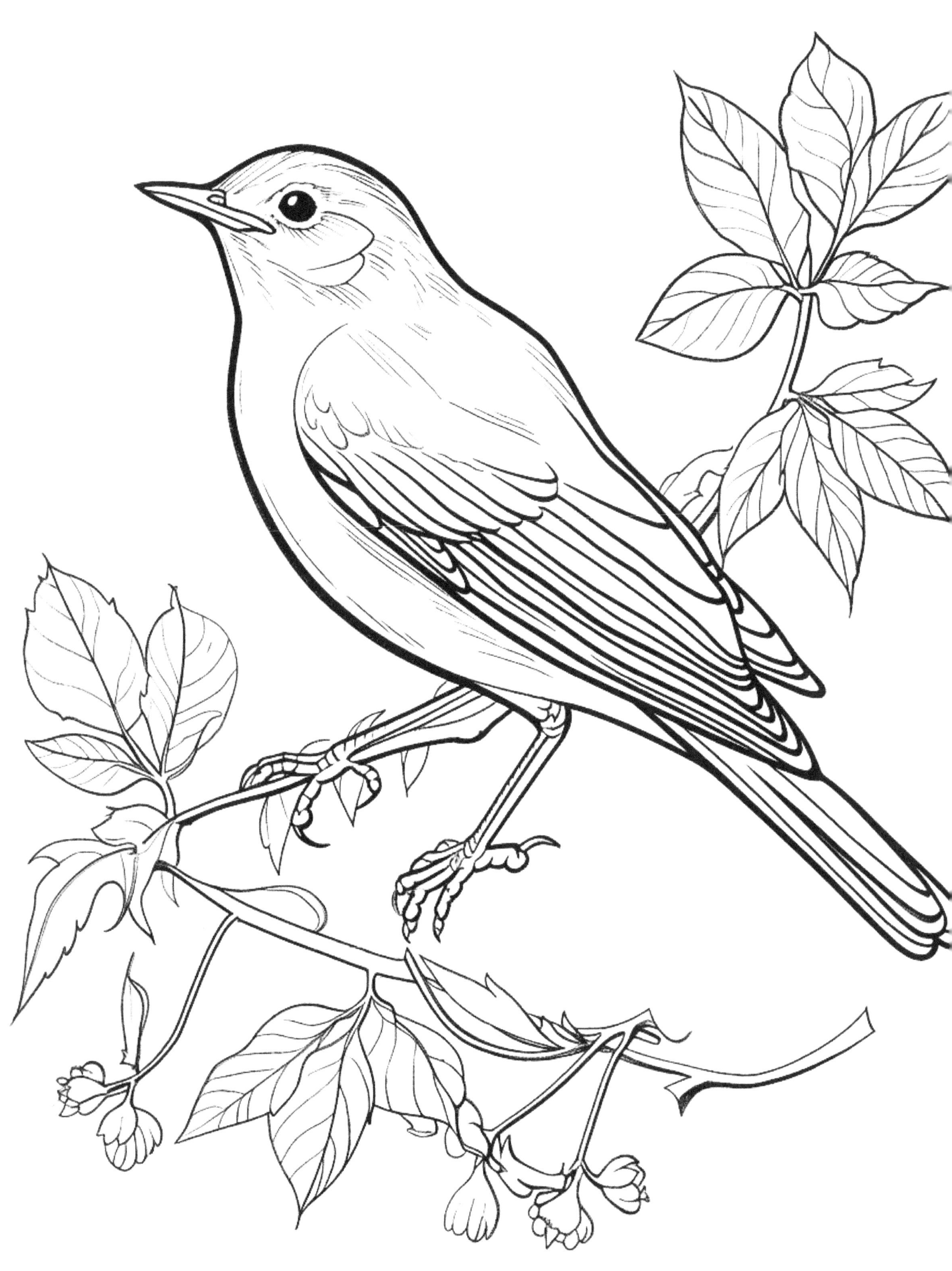

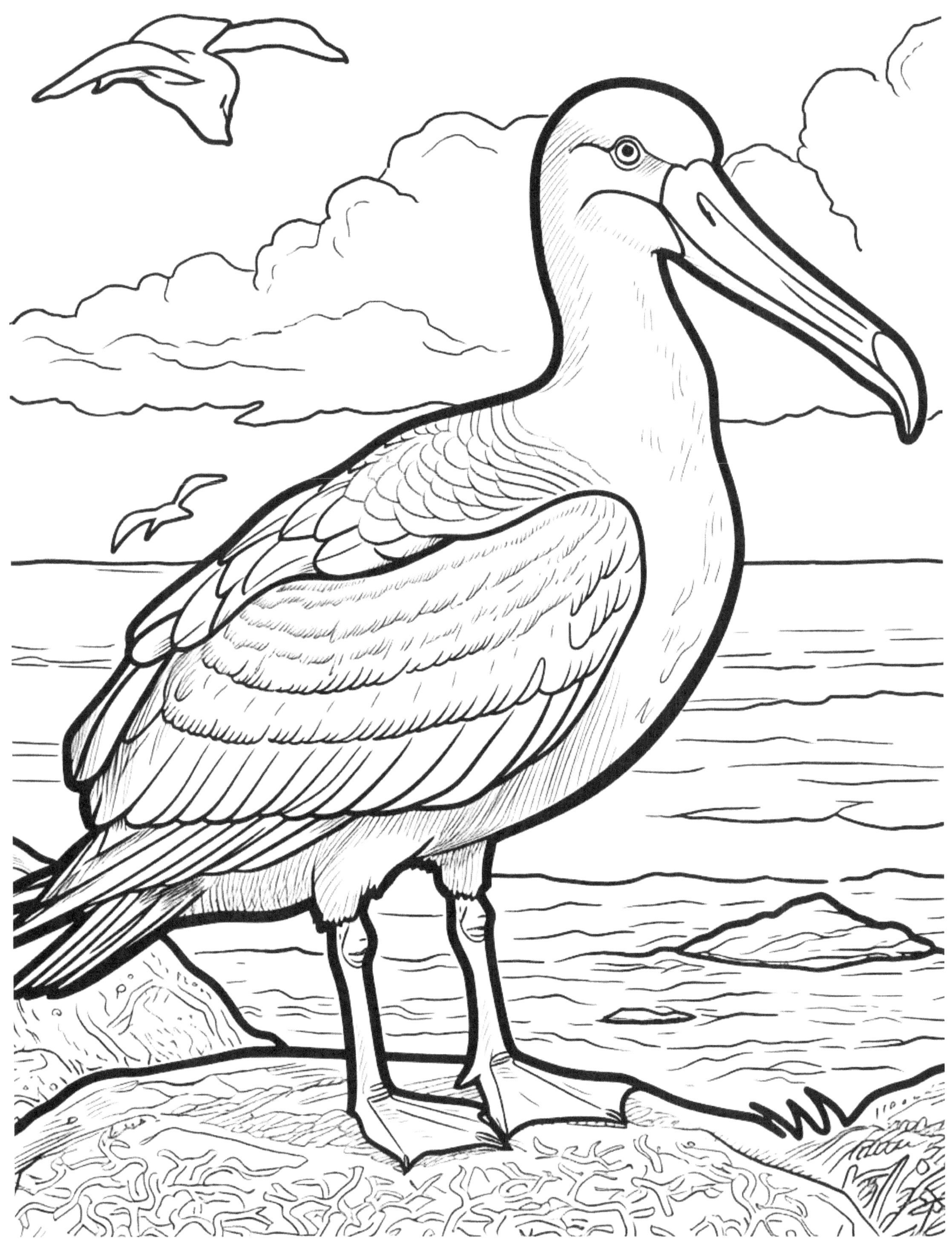

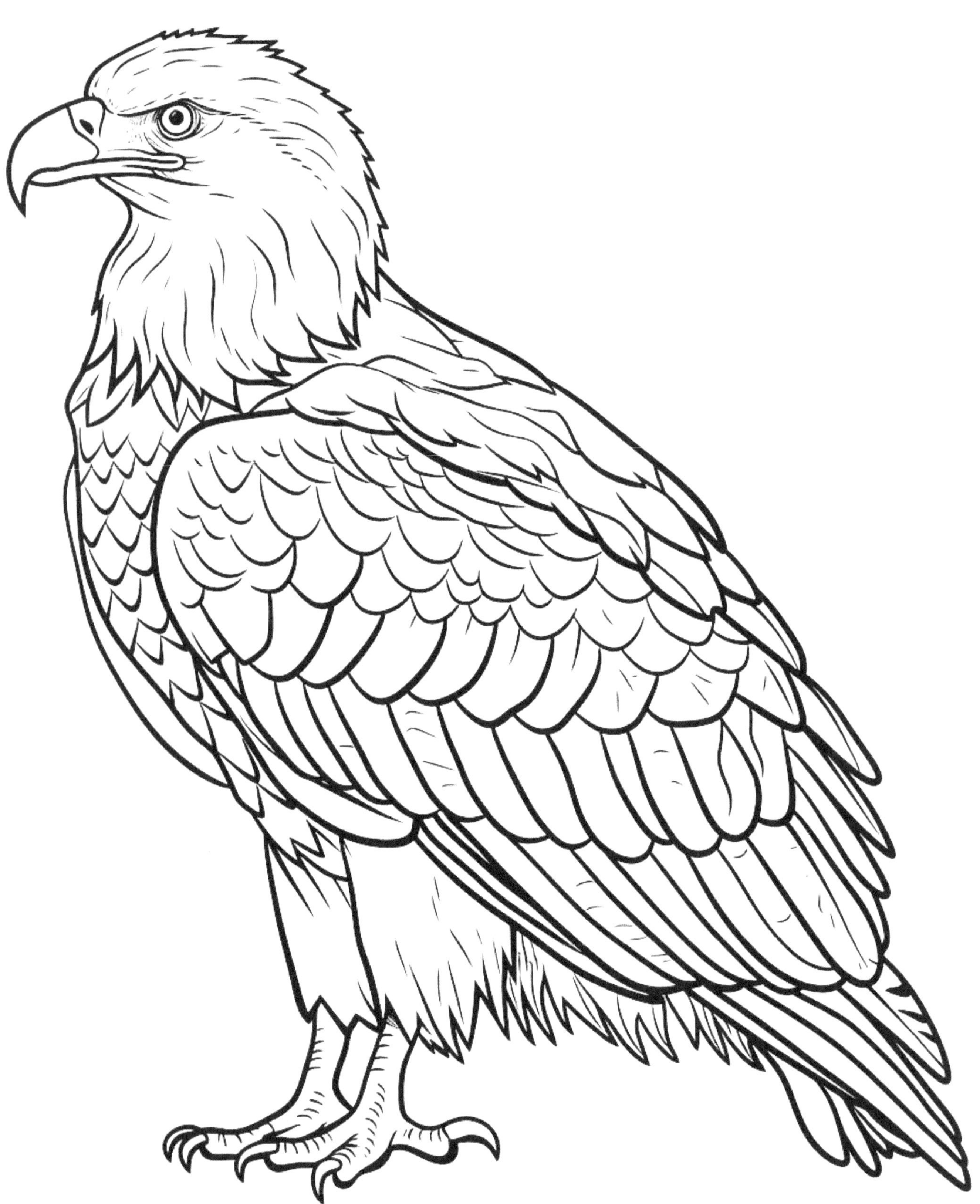

Thank you for taking flight with our feathered friends!

Your artistic touch has breathed life into these unique birds and their vibrant backgrounds.
I hope you enjoyed your coloring adventure!

Remember, the world is full of wonder, waiting to be explored and brought to life with your creativity.

Keep soaring, keep coloring, and keep sharing your artistic spirit!

Spread your wings and share your masterpieces! I'd love to see your colorful creations. Leave a review with your picture on Amazon.

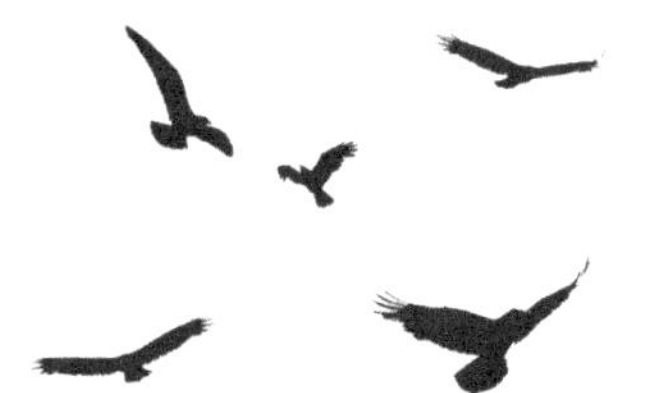